Talking to God

TALKING TO GOD
The Theology of Prayer

Wayne R. Spear

Crown & Covenant Publications
Pittsburgh, Pennsylvania

© 2002 Wayne R. Spear
Published by Crown & Covenant Publications
7408 Penn Avenue
Pittsburgh, PA 15208
www.psalms4u.com

First published, 1974
Second printing, 1979
Second edition, 2002

ISBN# 1-884527-13-2

Library of Congress Control Number: 2002107636

All Scripture quotations taken from the *New King James Version*,
© Thomas Nelson, Inc.

Page and cover design by Esther Howe. Text and heads are set
in Adobe Cochin, Avant Garde, and Hoefler Text Ornaments.

Printed in the USA by Faith & Life Press, Scottdale, PA.

Table of Contents

Foreword

In its original form, this book was done as a thesis for the Th.M. degree at Westminster Theological Seminary in Philadelphia. It was subsequently published by the Board of Christian Education and Publication of the Reformed Presbyterian Church (now Crown and Covenant) in 1974, then by Baker Book House in 1979.

This edition has been substantially revised, to make the book more readable for those who are not academically trained in theology. References to Hebrew and Greek words have been removed, and questions for discussion and reflection have been added, to make the book useful for study classes.

I want to express my gratitude to Professor Norman Shepherd, my advisor and mentor at Westminster Seminary, and to the editors of Crown and Covenant Publications, especially Esther Howe, for making the publication of this new edition possible.

I also want to express my thanks to my wife, Mary, who typed several drafts of the original project on a used standard typewriter (in pre-computer days). She has been my companion, helper, and encourager in all my work.

I send out this book with the prayer that the Lord will use it to stimulate and guide Christians to pray more fully, more faithfully, and more fervently.

Wayne R. Spear
Reformed Presbyterian Theological Seminary
Pittsburgh, Pennsylvania
February 2002

Introduction

There is no shortage of books on the subject of prayer. Any Christian bookstore or catalogue will offer many works on the subject. Popular books on prayer tend to be of two sorts: those that record remarkable experiences in prayer, and those that give instruction about the practice of prayer. Much that is helpful is contained in some of these books. There are also many books on prayer that contain teaching that is unbiblical, and harmful to true godliness. Christians need to exercise discernment in their effort to improve and deepen their prayer life.

There are not many works that seek to present a full biblical *theology* of prayer. Lest the reader be put off by the use of the term "theology," an explanation is needed. "Theology," in the best sense of the term, is just the effort to understand, as fully and accurately as possible, what the Bible teaches on a particular subject. Prayer is not an activity that bypasses the mind. There are aspects of prayer that go beyond our understanding (see Rom. 8:26), but understanding the truth is essential to all parts of the Christian life, including prayer. Addressing some distortions in the practice of prayer in the church at Corinth, the Apostle Paul wrote: "I will pray with the spirit, and I will also pray with the understanding." (1 Cor. 14:15). We are concerned about the will of God when we pray; we come to know the will of God when we are transformed by the renewing of our minds (Rom. 12:2). In a very helpful book on prayer, Robert Brownson writes,

> Have you ever thought about how our "theology" affects our praying? Our deepest convictions about God usually determine the way in which we call on Him. We venture to state it as an abiding principle: *As we believe, so we pray.* (*Courage to Pray*, p. 16)

The faith that comes to expression in prayer needs to be grounded in the Scripture. It is in the Scripture that we come to know the God to whom we pray, and in the Scripture we learn the way in which we are to draw near to God in prayer.

Although there is a need for a biblical theology of prayer, few of the standard theological textbooks give adequate treatment of the subject of prayer. John Calvin has a long section on prayer in the *Institutes* that is unsurpassed in its comprehensiveness, biblical insight, and devotional warmth (*Institutes of the Christian Religion*, III:XX). Charles Hodge has a short section on prayer in his *Systematic Theology*, devoted mainly to answering objections to the validity of prayer raised by modern unbelief (pp. 692-709). Careful theological studies of prayer from a Reformed standpoint are rare.

This book, though it is brief, seeks to present a fairly complete summary of what the Bible teaches about prayer. It is based upon the conviction that the Bible is God's Word, fully trustworthy in all that it teaches. The writer is committed to the theology of the Reformation. For the study of prayer, this means that the study is undertaken with a conscious awareness of the absolute sovereignty of God, and of His undeserved grace as the source of salvation. It involves studying Scripture in a certain way, seeking its meaning through study of words and grammatical structure, with an awareness of the unity and historical progression of God's revelation.

The teaching of the Bible about prayer is scattered throughout both Testaments, in literally hundreds of references. To identify these references, it is necessary to have in mind a preliminary definition of prayer, so that one will recognize a passage about prayer in Scripture even if the usual words for prayer are not used in that passage. Such a definition is given in the first chapter.

This book concentrates on teaching about prayer that is found in the New Testament. However, the New Testament constantly looks back on the events and teaching recorded in the Old Testament, and can be accurately understood only against that background. A brief consideration of prayer in the Old Testament is presented in Chapter Two.

As one attempts to understand the massive amount of teaching about prayer in the Bible, it becomes clear that prayer has both objective and subjective aspects. Prayer is based in reality, and the Bible gives us reliable teaching about that reality. This is what we mean when we speak of the objective aspects of prayer. They have to do with the nature and activity of God in relation to the world and the people He has created. The objective aspects of prayer are discussed in Chapters Three, Four, and Five of the book. The reader will notice that the study is divided along Trinitarian lines. This method of procedure not only has the benefit of long historical precedent (the Apostles' Creed is so organized), but the biblical material lends itself to such a division. Scripture refers to the distinctive roles of the Father, Son, and Spirit in relation to prayer.

Prayer also has important subjective aspects, since it involves personal communication with God regarding one's condition and circumstances. Chapters Six and Seven deal with these aspects, having to do with the qualifications in the one who prays, and with the content of proper prayer.

The biblical teaching about prayer gives rise to certain objections, both from without and from within the circle of faith. From the side of faith, the necessity of prayer is, tacitly at least, apt to be questioned. Skeptcism denies the efficacy of prayer, or else seeks "natural" explanation for it. The eighth chapter is occupied with the defense of prayer against these objections.

Throughout history, believers have wrestled with questions that arise regarding prayer, and there have always been skeptics and scoffers who have rejected prayer as a meaningful human activity. From the standpoint of the believer, it is the *necessity* of prayer that may be puzzling. If God is sovereign, and His purposes are eternal and unchangeable, then what difference does it make whether or not we pray? From the standpoint of unbelief, the *effectiveness* of prayer is challenged, or else a naturalistic explanation of the working of prayer is sought. Chapter Eight is given to the defense of prayer against these objections. A brief summary of the results of the scriptural study of prayer is given in Chapter Nine.

A study of theology itself will not make one a godly person. A study of the theology of prayer will not in itself make one persistent and powerful in prayer. However, *knowing the truth* is an essential part of making progress in godliness, and it is an essential part of learning to pray in the right way. The reader is encouraged to approach the study of this book, and of the Scripture passages that it discusses, with the attitude of the disciples who came to Jesus with the request, "Lord, teach us to pray" (Luke 11:1). Remember that

All Scripture is given by inspiration of God, and is profitable for doctrine, for reproof, for correction, for instruction in righteousness, that the man of God may be complete, thoroughly equipped for every good work. (2 Tim. 3:16-17)

The development of a rich, effective prayer life is a central component of what it is to be a mature and effective Christian, and the Scripture is given to us to instruct us in cultivating the "good work" of prayer.

May your study of this little book be used of God to that end.

Questions for Discussion and Reflection

✗ What meaning does the word "theology" have for you? Does the word have a positive or negative connotation? How does the book explain the meaning of "theology"?

✗ Do you think most Christians see a connection between prayer and theology? Why or why not? How does the book justify the connection?

✗ What difficulties do you face in your understanding and practice of prayer?

✗ List three of your favorite Bible passages on the subject of prayer.

Chapter One
The Definition of Prayer

When we begin to study the Bible to discover what it teaches about prayer, we already have some understanding about what prayer is. Otherwise, we would not recognize many passages in which information about prayer is given. We know about the human activity called prayer. As we read Scripture, we find the same kind of activity being referred to. By studying Scripture, our preliminary understanding of prayer will be corrected and enlarged; but without the preliminary understanding, our study could not begin at all. So it is necessary at the beginning of this study to give a provisional definition of the concept of prayer: *Prayer is human language that is addressed to God.*

It is a *human* activity that is under consideration. It may well be that angels pray; certainly Scripture tells us that they are engaged in worshiping God (Ps. 148:2). There might be something analogous to prayer in other creatures, as some psalms suggest in highly poetic language (Ps. 98, for example, where seas, rivers, and mountains are called upon to rejoice at the coming of the Lord). But our purpose is to apply the biblical teaching on prayer to ourselves as human beings created for conscious fellowship with God.

We call prayer *a form of language*. It is capable of being expressed in words, whether or not spoken aloud. Prayer may be distinguished on one hand from mere mental activity such as meditation. On the other hand, it is distinguished from bodily activity that cannot be translated into words. It is not always easy to find the dividing line between meditation and silent prayer, or between a gesture that may be a kind of language, and one that is not. But the distinction is real and important.

It may be said that meditation is a form of prayer, or that acts of charity are virtual prayers. No doubt, instances of the use of the word "prayer" in both ways could be found. Certainly Scripture encourages both meditation and Christian service. But the words for prayer are not applied in the Bible to such activities, and this indicates that we must focus our study on prayer as language: people *talking* to God.

Further, we speak here of prayer as language *addressed to God*. The English word "pray" is often used to refer to a request made by one human to another, and many examples of this kind of "prayer" are found in the Bible. However, there are important differences between requests and expressions of praise on a human level, and prayer which ascends from human worshipers to God. Our study deals with prayer in the latter sense.

When prayer is defined as language addressed to God, many kinds of speech are included. Language is not a purely intellectual activity. When we are confronted with the majesty and perfection of God, our proper response is *adoration*: "Yours, O Lord, is the greatness, the power and the glory, the victory and the majesty" (1 Chron. 29:11). When we reflect upon the blessings that God has given, we *give thanks*: "Oh give thanks to the LORD, for He is good! / for His mercy endures forever" (Ps. 136:1). Faced with the holiness of God, and aware of our own sinfulness, our prayer is one of *confession*: "Against You, You only, have I sinned, / and done *this* evil in Your sight" (Ps. 51:4). Reflection on the sovereignty and the goodness of God leads to the prayer of *submission*: "Into Your hand I commit my spirit; / You have redeemed me, O LORD God of truth" (Ps. 31:5). Love for God and confidence in His grace produce *commitment* to future obedience: "Then we will not turn back from You; / revive us and we will call upon Your name" (Ps. 80:18). A sense of need, a desire for the fullness of God's blessing, gives rise to heartfelt *petition*: "O Lord, hear! O Lord, forgive! O Lord, listen and act!" (Dan. 9:19).

Of all these forms of prayer—adoration, thanksgiving, confession, submission, commitment, and petition—the last is the kind of prayer most difficult to understand. The question of the proper content of prayer, and the questions regarding answers to prayer, are concerned primarily with prayer in the sense of petition: asking things from God. So this study of the theology of prayer will give special attention to the matter of petitionary prayer. Other aspects of prayer are also important, however. Perhaps one of our greatest problems in the practice of prayer is that we give almost all of our attention to *asking*, and neglect some of the more devotional aspects of prayer. We will attempt in this study to deal as fully as possible with the fullness of the Bible's teaching on prayer.

Questions for Discussion and Reflection

🗡   If you were to give a different definition of prayer from the one presented in this chapter, what would it be?

🗡   How does prayer differ from meditation?

✂ Six forms or aspects of prayer are named in this chapter. Would you add others to the list?

✂ Read Psalms 25–28, and identify the different forms of prayer that are expressed in them.

✂ Which kinds of prayer are easiest for you? Which form the largest part of your prayer life?

Chapter Two
The Old Testament Background

A proper view of the Bible involves recognizing that the whole Bible was given by divine inspiration, and also being aware that God's revelation is progressive. All the books of the Bible are authoritative and trustworthy, but we must distinguish between revelation that is incomplete and preparatory, and revelation that is full and final.

The Old and New Testaments are related to one another as preparation and fulfillment. Presenting as it does the revelation given in connection with the coming of the promised Savior, the New Testament is God's *final* written Word to us. That cannot be said of the Old Testament: "For the law was given through Moses, but grace and truth came through Jesus Christ" (John 1:17). "God, who at various times and in various ways spoke in time past to the fathers by the prophets, has in these last days spoken to us by His Son" (Heb. 1:1-2). Because this is so, the New Testament stands in the foreground, and the Old Testament in the background, of the study of the Bible's teaching on prayer. The New Testament provides knowledge about prayer not given in the Old Testament, especially with regard to the roles of the Son of God and the Holy Spirit in prayer. And in the light of the New Testament teaching, it is seen that some aspects of the practice of prayer in the Old Testament (for example, the connection between prayer and the Levitical priesthood and sacrifices) had only a temporary and typical significance, and are not to be followed in a literal way by Christian believers.

This does not mean that Old Testament teaching can be ignored in our study. The New Testament constantly assumes knowledge of what has gone before, and cannot be fully understood without some acquaintance with the Old Testament background. Therefore, without trying to present a full discussion of the doctrine and practice of prayer in the Old Testament, we will give some attention to certain topics drawn from the Old Testament. They have been chosen for their importance for understanding the New Testament's teaching about prayer.

General Characteristics

A "doctrine" of prayer may be drawn from what is implicit in the literature of the Old Testament. It is interesting to find, however, that there is a relatively small amount of explicit teaching about prayer in that part of the Bible. What there is is located mostly in the wisdom literature (Psalms and Proverbs, for example), and some of the prophetic books. There is a much larger amount of descriptive and narrative material, recording the occurrence and content of actual prayer by the people of God.

Statements about prayer in the Old Testament must be carefully weighed. All of the Bible is true, but we need to recognize that in some passages we are given an inspired record of fallible human reasoning about prayer. In Job 8:5-6, for example, Bildad assures Job that if he were pure and upright, God would answer his prayers and take away his misery. Yet when we study the Book of Job as a whole, we learn that Job's suffering, and God's seeming indifference, are not consequences of Job's sin, but are part of a spiritual conflict between God and Satan, of which Job is unaware. The secret to answered prayer is not so simple as Bildad thinks.

Historical accounts of prayer in the Old Testament also require that we pay careful attention to the context, and to the whole of biblical teaching. We must distinguish between examples of prayer that are patterns for us, on one hand, and, on the other hand, accounts that give us an accurate portrayal of prayer that is improper.

The Nature of Old Testament Prayer

Prayer in the Old Testament is an integral part of a loving, trusting, reverent relationship with God. Prayer is not regarded simply as a duty to be performed by a godly person. Rather, it is the expression in speech of the whole religious consciousness of the believer. It is not so much a part of piety, as piety itself coming to expression.

The inseparability of prayer from the religious life is indicated in a number of ways in the Old Testament. Strangely, there is no record of God instituting prayer, such as we have for the Sabbath and marriage (Gen. 2:2-3, 23-24). Apparently, Adam and Eve began to pray spontaneously. When the Law was given at Sinai, there was ratification of previously given revelation, and new revelation regarding God's will. Yet in that Law, the only explicit instruction regarding prayer is about the confession of sin (Lev. 5:5; 16:21; 26:40-42). The instruction about prayer that is given in the poetical and prophetic portions of the Old Testament deals with the proper ways in which prayer should be made. The Bible assumes that the godly will pray; it is only necessary that they be instructed how to pray in the right way.

Prayer arises spontaneously in a person who is conscious of his or her need, and of God's power and goodness. When people "say prayers" instead of *praying*, when there is a separation between prayer and life, then prayer is meaningless. When God sees the people "draw near Me with their mouths, and honor Me with their lips, but have removed their hearts far from Me, and their fear toward Me is taught by the commandment of men" (Isa. 29:13), then He promises judgment.

Prayer in the Old Testament is the expression of the religious consciousness of a person who does not exist in and of himself, but who is in a covenant relationship with the living God. Prayer is not a soliloquy, nor is it a magic incantation. Prayer is communication with the God who has revealed Himself by His word and in mighty acts of redemption for His people. Prayer involves a God who hears (Ps. 65:2); who is in control of all the events of history (Isa. 44:24–45:8); who does not act arbitrarily, but in accordance with His own nature (Gen 18:25) and in fulfillment of His promises (Ps. 105:8-11). He has promised to respond to the prayers of His people (2 Chron. 7:14-15). Prayer that rests upon such convictions is not a late development in the Old Testament, but is present in the earliest period of time recorded.

The Content of Old Testament Prayer

There are some people who hold a negative view of the Old Testament. They believe that it is not only incomplete because of its earlier place in the history of redemption, but that it also presents characteristics that are improper, requiring correction in the light of the New Testament. Isaac Watts defended the introduction of his hymns into the worship of the church by asserting the unsuitability of the Old Testament psalms for use as Christian praise:

> While we are kindling into Divine Love by the Meditations of the loving Kindness of God...within a few Verses some dreadful Curse against Men is propos'd to our Lips...which is...contrary to the Commandment, of loving our Enemies. (*Isaac Watts: Hymns and Spiritual Songs, 1707-1748, p. lii*)

Because of this popular but mistaken belief, we need to examine the content of Old Testament prayer.

First of all, there is prayer for *divine guidance*. One of the earliest recorded prayers is that of Abraham's servant Eliezer, in which he prays for direction in finding a wife for his master's son (Gen. 24:12-14). Very frequently in the Old Testament believers pray for guidance from God. This is a recurring petition in the Psalms: "Cause me to know the way in which I should walk, / for I lift up my soul to You" (Ps. 143:8).

Request for *provision* is another frequent prayer:

> They wandered in the wilderness in a desolate way;
> They found no city to dwell in.
> Hungry and thirsty,
> Their soul fainted in them.
> Then they cried out to the LORD in their trouble,
> *And* He delivered them out of their distresses. (Ps. 107:4-6)

The reference in this psalm is to the Exodus. Over and over, Israel prayed for provision of water and food, and their prayers were answered.

There is also prayer for *deliverance* from disease, and from such natural dangers as storms at sea. Hezekiah was granted an additional 15 years of life in response to such a prayer (2 Kings 20:1-6). On the other hand, Asa is criticized for failing to seek the Lord with regard to his disease (2 Chron. 16:12). In the face of the uncertainty of the future, of the need for food and shelter, of the threat of natural disaster, the Old Testament believer sought for God's help through prayer. But more prominent than all these, in the Old Testament, is prayer for deliverance from enemies—and for their destruction. This is strikingly expressed in the words of Moses that punctuated Israel's journey through the wilderness: "Whenever the ark set out...Moses said, 'Rise up, O LORD! Let Your enemies be scattered, and let those who hate You flee before You'" (Num. 10:35). The Psalms are filled with passages in which pleas for God's mercies are inseparably linked with petitions for the pouring out of His wrath upon the enemies of the psalmist, and of Israel (for example, Ps. 94). Because of such prayers, some have constructed a view of Old Testament prayer that regards it as materialistic, nationalistic, selfish, and unspiritual—as an effort to manipulate God to the advantage of an individual, or of a nation greedy for conquest. It is not to be denied that individuals in the Old Testament (as now), and Israel as a whole, at times fell short of a proper understanding of their relationship to God, of the necessity to love their enemies, and of the purpose of prayer. Nevertheless, to brand Old Testament prayer generally as "unChristian" ignores several important considerations.

There is much prayer in the Old Testament that does not refer primarily to temporal benefits, but to the favor of God as such. A rich strand of prayer in the Book of Psalms recognizes the possession of God's favor as surpassing all other good things: "Because Your lovingkindness *is* better than life, / my lips shall praise You" (Ps. 63:3). Perplexity over the prosperity of the wicked finds its solution in recognizing the supreme value of knowing God and enjoying fellowship with Him (Ps. 73; Hab. 3:17-19). It is this desire for God's favor which leads to the prayer of penitence that is so common throughout the Old Testament: "Do not cast me away from Your presence, / And do not take Your Holy Spirit from me. / Restore to me the joy of Your salvation" (Ps. 51:11-12).

The prominence of this aspect of prayer enables us to place prayer for temporal blessings in proper perspective. In its better moments, at least, Israel, instructed by the covenant promises of Deuteronomy 28, regarded temporal blessings as indications of God's favor. Famine, disease, and oppression by enemies were all instruments used by God to chasten His people for their sin. Prayer for relief from these calamities was at the same time prayer for forgiveness and restoration to fellowship with God. Periods of short-lived repentance, as during the time of the Judges, indicated that at times escape from temporal misery was the prime motive for prayer. But there were other instances where it was primarily the renewal of God's favor that was sought. The thirsting for God expressed in Psalms 42 and 43 is an appropriate example.

Beyond this, it must be seen that because Israel was a nation chosen by God to have a special role in carrying out His purpose of redemption, the enemies of Israel were also the enemies of God. Even the pleas of individuals for vengeance must be understood in this perspective. The one who prays for God's judgment on his enemies is a member of the covenant people. In a number of the imprecatory ("cursing") psalms, the one who prays stands at the head of Israel as king. Therefore prayers for God's judgment in the Old Testament should not be regarded as expressions of personal hatred. They utter the desire that God may be glorified in the success of His purposes and in the defeat of His enemies. We should also realize that the *New* Testament speaks of vengeance coming upon the enemies of God. The martyrs in heaven are pictured, in Revelation 6:10, as waiting for God to judge and avenge their blood. The teaching of the New Testament as well as the Old, is *not* that there is no vengeance, but that righteous vengeance belongs to the Lord (Rom. 12:19).

The content of Old Testament prayer, then, is not limited to the desire for temporal welfare. There is a deeper quest for the enjoyment of God's favor both in this life and in the life to come. There is also the fervent desire that God may be glorified in the accomplishment of His purpose in the world.

Prayer and Sacrifice

To understand Old Testament piety, we need to consider the relationship between prayer and the offering of sacrifices to God.

There was no rigid rule in the Old Testament that prayer must always be accompanied by sacrifice. Examples of prayer without specific mention of sacrifice occur in early times (Gen. 24:12-14; 32:9-12), after the giving of the Law (Num. 14:13-19), and during the Babylonian Captivity, when no sacrifices could be offered at all (Dan. 9:3-19). It would certainly be the case that there was a continual practice of personal and family devotion which was not directly connected with the ceremonies of the Tabernacle or the Temple. When the psalmist speaks of praying three times a day (Ps. 55:17), we should not think that he went to the sanctuary to offer sacrifice that often.

However, there was a strong connection between prayer and sacrifice in the time before Christ. The sanctuary and the sacrifices were seldom absent from the mind of the Israelites when they prayed.

Prayer and sacrifice occurred together when Abraham "built an altar to the LORD, and called on the name of the Lord" (Gen. 12:8). Job prayed for his friends as they offered their sacrifices (Job 42:8–9). In the Mosaic ceremonies, confession of sin accompanied the sin offering (Lev. 5:5; 16:21). David made provision for congregational singing, which is a form of prayer, in connection with the sacrificial ritual (1 Chron. 16).

Songs of thanksgiving were sung as sacrifices were offered at the dedication of the rebuilt wall of Jerusalem (Neh. 12:31-43).

During times of exile from Jerusalem, the sanctuary remained precious to God's people (see Ps. 42 and 43). Daniel's custom of praying with his window open toward Jerusalem (Dan. 6:10) is an indication of how prayer was linked to the place of sacrifice. Solomon's prayer at the dedication of the Temple would be in Daniel's mind:

> And when they return to You with all their heart and with all their soul in the land of their captivity, where they have been carried captive, and pray toward...the temple which I have built for Your name: then hear from heaven Your dwelling place their prayer and their supplications. (2 Chron. 6:38-39)

Prayer was to be directed toward the Temple, not because God was physically located there (see 2 Chron. 6:18), but because it was the place of sacrifice: "I have heard your prayer, and have chosen this place for Myself as a house of sacrifice" (2 Chron 7:12).

Daniel could pray even though no sacrifice was then being offered. But he prayed with the memory of the sacrificial ritual of the Temple in his thoughts. As the New Testament confirms, this means that while prayer in the Old Testament did not depend for its efficacy upon animal sacrifices, the sacrificial system was instituted by God to teach His people that as sinners they could approach Him only by way of the Atonement.

Even when prayer seems to be placed in contrast to sacrifice, as in Psalms 50 and 51, we should not see this as the replacement of sacrifice by prayer. Rather, it is the formal offering of sacrifice without real contrition of heart that is being rejected. Where the right heart attitude is lacking, God has no delight in sacrifice. But when there has been repentance and restoration to God's favor, then God will "be pleased with the sacrifices of righteousness, / With burnt offering and whole burnt offering" (Ps. 51:19).

Thus prayer and sacrifice in the Old Testament were complementary. Sacrifice was not an erroneous way of approaching God, but vividly set forth the only way in which sinful people could approach a holy God, namely by way of the shedding of the blood of a divinely-provided substitute. Whether praying in the Temple courtyard or by the rivers of Babylon, the believing Israelite was conscious of the need for a covering for sin. He or she prayed depending upon the promise of a Savior who was yet to come, whose saving work was portrayed in the rituals of the Temple.

Intercession in the Old Testament

The ceremonial rituals of the Old Testament also set forth the need for a mediator or intercessor, in approaching God.

The role of the intercessor in the patriarchal age was performed by the head of the family (see Job. 1:5). Under the Law of Moses, a hereditary priesthood was established in the family of Aaron, by whom sacrifices were ordinarily to be offered (Ex. 28–29). The clearest indication of the priest's role as intercessor was seen in the burning of incense upon the golden altar (Ex. 30:1-10). The incense was the symbol of prayer ascending to God (see Ps. 141:2; Rev. 5:8). It was burned morning and evening by the priests, as "a perpetual incense before the Lord" (Ex. 30:8). The Israelites, praying in their dwellings, remembered that in the sanctuary the priest was burning incense before the Lord on their behalf. So there was presented to their minds the concept of a divinely provided mediator, making prayer for them continually.

The figure of the intercessor appears in other ways in the Old Testament. The history of the covenant people was in itself a revelation that looked forward to the coming of the Messiah. In the history of Israel the function of intercession was often performed by one who stood at the head of God's people.

Abraham interceded with God for the righteous who were threatened with destruction in wicked Sodom (Gen. 18:22-32). Moses, the leader of Israel, prayed over and over again for provision and mercy on behalf of his wayward people (Ex. 15:25; 17:4; 32:11-14; 34:8-9). Israel was so dependent on Samuel's prayers that even when they refused to be ruled by God through him, they sought his intercession for them (1 Sam. 12:19, 23). David and Solomon, as kings, uttered memorable prayers for their people (1 Chron. 29:10-19; 2 Chron. 6:12-42). In times of revival, Asa, Jehoshaphat, and Hezekiah interceded with the Lord for Israel (2 Chron. 14:11; 20:5-12; 30:18-20). During and after the Exile, Daniel and Ezra appeared as leaders who prayed for the suffering remnant of God's chosen people (Dan. 9:3-19; Ezek. 9:5-15).

From this long tradition of the ruler who was also intercessor, later generations understood Isaiah's prophecy regarding the Suffering Servant who would make "intercession for the transgressors" (Isa. 53:12). The New Testament references to Christ's priestly work of intercession are illuminated by this background.

Questions for Discussion and Reflection

↗ Do any of the Ten Commandments give teaching about prayer? Explain.

↗ How do you respond to the statement that Old Testament prayer was mainly for earthly prosperity? How should we pray about temporal matters?

↗ What should a Christian think about the Old Testament prayers for the destruction of enemies? Should we pray in the same way?

↗ Why was prayer in the Old Testament often connected to the offering of sacrifice?

↗ In what ways was Israel taught the need for an intercessor?

Chapter Three
The One to Whom We Pray

The Attributes of God

Prayer according to the Bible is not a purely human activity. It is personal communication that is addressed to the living God. Prayer does not begin with us, but with God. He is at work in us to cause us to desire and then to do what pleases Him (Phil. 2:12-13). He moves us to pray.

When we make requests of God, we look for His working in events and persons beyond ourselves, as we anticipate His answers to our prayers. Thus prayer has its basis in the nature and activity of God, and is meaningful only because of that reality. In a memorable passage about prayer (Mark 11:22-24) Jesus began by saying, "Have faith in God!" What is it that we must know and believe about God in order to pray in the right way?

Prayer is a form of human communication that differs from other language just because it is addressed to God. We might address a plea for help or a request for forgiveness to another human being, and might even use similar words in doing so, but that is quite different from praying. Prayer to God, if it is offered in faith, takes into account what God has revealed to us about His own nature. We will see what a difference this makes as we think about the attributes of God that are most important for prayer.

God is all-knowing and everywhere present.

A plea addressed to another human being depends upon factors of space and time in order to be heard. Response to our call can come only from one who can be reached by sound waves, or electronic communication, or by letter. In addition, there are limitations of language. A request for help might be ignored because it is spoken to those speaking a different language, or sent to those who cannot read.

Prayer to God is different because it does not have such limitations. The infinite, all-knowing God is able to hear and understand, no matter what language we speak, or what the circumstances are in which the prayer is made. David was confident of God's ability to hear, even though he prayed "from the end of the earth" (Ps. 61:2). At the dedication of the Temple, Solomon recognized that God could not be localized in any place of worship, but that He would hear prayer from heaven (2 Chron. 6:18, 21). Prayer would be heard even when made from the battlefield, or from the land of captivity (2 Chron. 6:34, 38). Elijah ironically advised the prophets of Baal to pray loudly, since their god might be at a distance, or preoccupied, or asleep (1 Kings 18:27). His words implied that it would be absurd to think of the living God in such a way. He is the one who "shall neither slumber nor sleep" (Ps. 121:4).

Jesus connected the omniscience of God to prayer when He taught that men should pray privately to their Father "who sees in secret" (Matt. 6:6). The quiet prayer of the believer, uttered in a private place, does not escape the notice of God.

Because God is omniscient, that is, that He knows all things, prayer must be offered in sincerity, from the heart. Since "there is no creature hidden from His sight, but all things are naked and open to the eyes of Him to whom we must give account" (Heb. 4:13), there is no possibility that mere words, or the formal act of praying in itself, will induce a favorable response from God. It is because God is omniscient, according to Jesus' teaching, that the "vain repetitions" characteristic of the prayers of unbelievers, are of no value before God (Matt. 6:7).

God is all-powerful.

Prayer to God is further distinguished from language addressed to human beings because the power of its Hearer is unlimited.

The psalmist expresses the contrast between the help to be expected from the most powerful of human beings, who are finite, and from the infinite God, in a striking way:

> Do not put your trust in princes,
> *Nor* in a son of man, in whom *there is* no help.
> His spirit departs, he returns to his earth;
> In that very day his plans perish.
> Happy *is he* who *has* the God of Jacob for his help,
> Whose hope *is* in the LORD his God,
> Who made heaven and earth,
> The sea, and all that *is* in them;
> Who keeps truth forever.... (Ps. 146:3–6)

The prayer of faith is addressed to God, "who is able to do exceedingly abundantly above all that we ask or think" (Eph. 3:20). The angel who came to announce the impending birth of John the Baptist told his father Zacharias that his prayer for a son was heard. Yet, because he and Elizabeth had passed the usual age for having children, Zacharias did not believe the message from God. Because of his lack of faith, his power of speech was taken away until the child was born. The birth of John was a demonstration of the fact that "with God nothing will be impossible" (Luke 1:37). If we pray with biblical faith, we will not set limits upon what God is *able* to do.

Praying in faith means responding to what the Scripture tells us about the God *who is able*. He is "able to make all grace abound" toward us (2 Cor. 9:8). He is able "to keep [us] from stumbling, and to present us faultless before the presence of His glory" (Jude 24). It is to the God of unlimited power that we direct our prayer.

God is the providential ruler of creation.

The distinctiveness of prayer addressed to God also comes from the fact that He actively controls and directs everything that happens in the world. Other creatures have only a secondary and limited role in the occurrence of particular events, but the God to whom we pray is the one who "works all things according to the counsel of His will" (Eph. 1:11). Prayer, according to the Bible, is based upon belief in God's providential control over the world. According to the *Westminster Shorter Catechism*, providence is God's "most holy, wise and powerful preserving and governing all His creatures and all their actions" (Q. 11).

Apart from belief in providence, prayer would be limited to worshiping God for what He is in Himself, and thanking Him for His wisdom and bounty as shown in the original creation of the world. Yet everywhere in Scripture there are prayers of thanksgiving for God's wonderful works in history, and petitions for His gracious and just activity in the near and distant future.

Only a few examples of this need to be given. David's prayer in designating Solomon to succeed him includes a recognition of God's providence:

> Yours, O LORD, is the greatness, the power and the glory, the victory and the majesty; for all that is in heaven and in earth is Yours; Yours is the kingdom, O LORD, and You are exalted as head over all. Both riches and honor come from You, and You reign over all....Now therefore, our God, we thank You, and praise Your glorious name. (1 Chron. 29:11-13)

Nebuchadnezzar, the proud ruler of the Babylonian Empire, was taught to recognize God's sovereignty even over world leaders when God drove him from his throne by inflicting seven years of insanity on him. Upon his restoration he praised God, for:

> He does according to His will in the army of heaven, and among the inhabitants of the earth. No one can restrain His hand, or say to Him, "What have You done?" (Dan. 4:35)

The variety of requests made to God in biblical prayer indicates that His control extends over all events. Prayer recognizes Him as the one who gives daily food (Matt. 6:30-33); as the source of orderly government and peaceful society (1 Tim. 2:1-2); as the controller of circumstances that would permit Paul's journey to Rome (Rom. 1:9-10); as the source of the increasing holiness of believers (Phil. 1:9-11). Events in the natural world, conditions of human society, and developments in human personality are all ultimately under the control of God. If this were not so, it would be useless to pray about such things.

It is instructive to study prayers of thanksgiving in the Bible, to see how they support the doctrine of God's sovereignty. The Apostle Paul recorded his thankfulness to God for the election, the conversion, and the sanctification of believers in Thessalonica (1 Thess. 1:2-7; 2:13-14). Indeed, he exhorts them that in everything they are to give thanks (5:18), indicating that they are to see God's good hand in every experience of life.

God possesses ultimate authority over us.

Biblical prayer acknowledges God as the supreme lawgiver and judge, the one to whom we are ultimately responsible. His authority over us is complete.

Consciousness of the supreme authority of God leads to the prayer of unconditional commitment. A bare belief in God's pervasive control of the world could lead to passive submission, but the prayers of the Bible go beyond that. God's will is acknowledged to be *good*, and the revelation of that will is adopted as the standard for the believer's life. In a psalm that celebrates the power of God in creation, and in the affairs of rulers and nations, the moral perfection of God's rule is acknowledged:

> For the word of the LORD *is* right,
> And all His work is *done* in truth.
> He loves righteousness and justice;
> The earth is full of the goodness of the LORD. (Ps 33:4-5)

The realization that "Our God *is* in heaven; / He does whatever He pleases" (Ps. 115:3) calls for us to place our trust in Him (Ps. 115:10-11). The prayer of Jesus in Gethsemane, "Your will be done" (Matt. 26:42), was not a statement of mere resignation, but of dedication. He came to do the will of His Father, and in that great spiritual struggle in the garden He continued to be obedient. He rose from prayer to go to the Cross. The petition of the Lord's Prayer, "Your will be done on earth as it is in heaven" (Matt. 6:10) is also to be understood as an expression of commitment. That is how Answer 124 of the *Heidelberg Catechism* understands it:

> That is, grant that we and all men may renounce our own will and obey Thy will, which alone is good, without grumbling, so that everyone may carry out his office and calling as willingly and faithfully as the angels in heaven.

When we adopt God's will as the standard of life and conduct, we become conscious of our failure to do God's will, and thus we must pray for the forgiveness of our sins: "For Your name's sake, O LORD, / Pardon my iniquity, for it *is* great" (Ps. 25:11). This sense of ultimate responsibility to God is another element that distinguishes prayer to God from other forms of address. The loyalty pledged to another person must always be less than one's ultimate allegiance to the will of God: "We ought to obey God rather than men" (Acts 5:29). And while a request for forgiveness can and should be made to fellow humans whom we have offended, it remains true that in the ultimate sense only God can forgive sins (Mark 2:7). David had grievously wronged both Uriah and Bathsheba by his adultery, yet he was led to pray to God, "Against You, You only, have I sinned, / And done *this* evil in Your sight" (Ps. 51:4). Forgiveness in the deepest sense comes only from God.

Thus, prayer is a unique form of human language because of the uniqueness of the one to whom it is addressed. Prayer in the Bible assumes, and often explicitly asserts, that God is omniscient and omnipresent; that His power is unlimited, that He is actively at work in the world, controlling and directing all events, and that He is the one to whom we are finally answerable. Because this is true, prayer is to be made to God alone. It is a part of that worship and service that is to be offered exclusively to the living God (Matt. 4:10).

The distinctiveness of prayer addressed to God as compared with speech directed to other human beings provides us a basis on which we can consider two questions that arise concerning the person(s) to whom prayer should be made. The first has to do with the invocation of saints; the second, with the doctrine of the Trinity.

The Invocation of Saints

Many of the Reformed Confessions emphasize that prayer is to be made to God alone. For example, the *Second Helvetic Confession* says:

> Since we do believe in God alone, we assuredly call upon
> Him alone, and we do so through Christ. For this reason we do
> not adore, worship, or pray to the saints in heaven, or to other
> gods, and we do not acknowledge them as our intercessors or
> mediators before the Father in heaven. (Chap. V)

Statements such as this were directed against the Roman Catholic practice of the invocation and veneration of the saints.

The Roman Catholic Church was sensitive to the charge of
idolatry that was being applied by the Protestants to these prac-
tices. In the Council of Trent the Catholics stated that

> they think impiously who deny that the saints who enjoy eternal
> happiness in heaven are to be invoked, or who assert that they do
> not pray for man, or that our invocation of them to pray for each of
> us is idolatry. (*Canons and Decrees of the Council of Trent,* Session 25)

Strictly speaking, the invocation of saints was understood to be
requesting their prayers, not praying to them directly for help.
It was defended as an extension of the unquestioned practice of
asking other Christians for their help in prayer.

The Reformers objected to the *theory* of the invocation and
veneration of saints on the grounds that it lacked positive biblical warrant. The charge of idolatry was based on the conviction
that, in *practice*, prayers to the saints involved ascribing to them
what belonged to God alone. John Calvin states his judgment
that "there are very many who do not refrain from the horrid
sacrilege of calling upon the saints now not as helpers but as
determiners of their salvation....How much farther has this dev-
ilish insolence spread, when men do not hesitate to transfer to
the dead what properly belongs to God and Christ?" (*Institutes,*
III:21-22). The Council of Trent as much as acknowledged that
such mistaken views were common, when they called upon
Catholics to remove "all superstition" from the invocation of
saints.

The invocation of saints was rightly termed idolatry because
by its very nature it blurred the clear distinction between prayer

to the Most High God, and speech addressed to human beings. The saints whose help is sought are understood to be in heaven, out of reach of ordinary human communication. Yet they are presumed to be able, like God, to "hear in heaven." Further, the Roman Catholic doctrine about sainthood, requiring for those declared to be enrolled as saints that miracles be worked in response to prayer addressed to them, made it very easy to attribute supernatural power to the saints. Events were thought to be under the control of various saints, rather than under the sovereignty of God. As Calvin says, "Then each man adopted a particular saint as a tutelary deity, in whose keeping he put his trust" (*Institutes*, XX:22). Anyone who thinks that views like these have disappeared should examine the classified ads in the local newspaper: ads praising St. Jude and other "saints" (including Baby[!] Jesus) for answering prayer appear almost every day.

Because such abuses are inherent in the invocation of saints, the rule must be maintained that prayer is to be made to God alone.

Prayer and the Doctrine of the Trinity

The Bible clearly teaches that God is to be the exclusive object of worship, and the one to whom alone we pray. Against this background, one of the strongest arguments for the full deity of Jesus Christ is that we are not only taught in the Bible to pray to God the Father, but we are also instructed to pray to the Son of God as well.

Perhaps the essential deity of Jesus was not always recognized by those who made requests of Him during His earthly ministry. The father of the epileptic boy had doubts about Jesus' ability to help even while he appealed to Him: "But if You can do anything, have compassion on us and help us" (Mark 9:22). Even though Martha confessed Jesus to be the

Messiah, she did not look for help to come from Him directly, but was confident that His prayer would be heard by God (John 11:22, 27).

Nevertheless, Jesus encouraged people to look to Him directly for help. When the commanding officer of a Roman military unit recognized that Jesus was one possessing authority, who needed only to "speak a word" for his servant to be healed, Jesus commended his faith (Matt. 8:5-13). A paralyzed man was brought to Him for healing, and Jesus saw his deeper need, and forgave his sins. The Jewish teachers who were present rightly understood that Jesus was claiming for Himself a power that belonged exclusively to God, the power to forgive sins (Matt. 9:2-7). In the fierce storm on Lake Galilee the disciples addressed their plea for help to Him: "Lord, save us! We are perishing!" In response, Jesus commanded the storm to cease, and there was a great calm (Matt. 8:24-27). In their wonder over His power, the disciples could hardly have failed to note the similarity between this power and that which belongs to God, of whom it is written that "Fire and hail, snow and clouds, stormy wind [fulfill] His word" (Ps. 148:8). In such incidents Jesus was encouraging His followers to pray to *Him* for the kind of help that could only come from God.

Jesus not only taught by implication that prayer should be made to Him; He stated it explicitly. We must understand His beautiful invitation in Matthew 11:28 as calling us to pray to Him: "Come to Me, all you who labor and are heavy laden, and I will give you rest." In the previous verse, Jesus had spoken of His relationship with His Father, so that the personal distinction between the Father and the Son is clearly in view. Jesus exhorts the weary to come to Him, and states with emphasis that *He* will grant them rest. The "coming" clearly implies prayer—the prayer of commitment, the prayer of petition for rest.

Another such passage is John 14:14: "If you ask *Me* anything in My name, I will do it." While the word "Me" is not found in all manuscripts of the passage, it is strongly supported by the textual evidence, and is appropriate because of the strong emphasis placed on the pronoun "I" at the end of the verse, as indicated by the Greek. Jesus here points to Himself as the one to whom prayer is to be addressed, and promises that He will answer.

There is a statement in John 16:23 that seems to deny that prayer is to be addressed to Jesus after His resurrection: "In that day you will ask Me nothing...whatever you ask the Father in My name, He will give you." The Greek words used, however, indicate that the contrast is not between asking the Father as opposed to asking the Son. Instead, the contrast is in the kind of asking. Jesus is speaking about a request for information (see v. 19). Because of the fullness of revelation that will be given with the sending of the Holy Spirit, there will no longer need to be this kind of request for information.

As a result of such teaching by Jesus, believers in the New Testament are found addressing prayer to Jesus Christ, explicitly ascribing to Him what belongs to God alone. After the resurrection, Thomas addresses Him as "My Lord and my God!" and Jesus responds by pronouncing a blessing on him (John 20:28-29). Peter did not hesitate to attribute omniscience to Jesus: "Lord, You know all things" (John 21:17). Stephen, the first martyr of the church, went to his death commending his spirit to Jesus (Acts 7:59; see Ps. 31:5). The common expression for prayer, "calling upon the name of the Lord," is used to speak of prayer addressed to the Son (Acts 9:21).

The teaching of the Scripture on prayer, then, requires that prayer be made to God alone, and yet it also indicates that prayer may be made to more than one person. The solution to this seeming paradox is to be found in the Christian doctrine of the

Trinity. B. B. Warfield summarized the biblical teaching on this subject in one clear sentence:

> We may show that the New Testament everywhere insists on the unity of the Godhead; that it constantly recognizes the Father as God, the Son as God, and the Spirit as God; and that it cursorily presents these three to us as distinct Persons. (*Biblical and Theological Studies*, p. 35)

The fact that Father, Son, and Spirit are distinct Persons means that such a distinction exists between them that they can know one another (Matt. 11:27); the Son can pray to the Father (Matt. 11:25; John 14:16); the Father commands the Son (John 14:31); the Spirit is sent by the Father and Son (John 14:16), and bears witness regarding the Son (John 15:26).

The famous modern theologian, Paul Tillich, wrote that the doctrine of the Trinity should be rejected because of the insuperable problems it poses for the practice of prayer. To believe in three distinct Persons, he charged, would lead to tritheism, the worship of three gods (*Systematic Theology*, III, p. 289). But if we submit, as we must, to God's self-revelation in the Bible, we will not limit God to what our human reason can fully understand. To Tillich's scornful question, whether prayer to one of the three Persons is directed to someone different from another of the three, we may answer affirmatively, if "different" means "capable of being distinguished from another." But if "different" means "separate" or "altogether different," then the question must be answered negatively. Probably no better description can be found of the way in which the Trinity is to be perceived than that which Calvin attributes to Gregory of Nazianzus:

> I cannot think on the one without quickly being encircled by the splendor of the three; nor can I discern the three without being straightway carried back to the one. (*Institutes*, I:XIII:17)

A prayer addressed to the Father does not regard Him as existing or acting in isolation from the Son and Spirit; only, for the moment, the First Person is in the focus of attention.

The very passages in the Bible that speak of a distinction of Persons stress the unity of God. Just before designating Himself as the one who would answer prayer, Jesus describes the essential oneness that He shares with the Father: "No one knows the Son except the Father. Nor does anyone know the Father except the Son" (Matt. 11:27). "Believe Me that I am in the Father, and the Father in Me" (John 14:11).

A practical question arises at this point. In terms of biblical teaching, is prayer to be addressed to the triune God, to each of the Persons equally, or to one of the Persons in distinction from the others? To put the question another way, since differences of function are assigned to the three Persons (as will be shown more fully later on), does the role of Hearer of prayer belong more to one of the Persons than to the others?

We have already seen that Scripture gives examples and commands that prayer is to be addressed to the Son as well as to the Father. This is in harmony with the view that each of the Persons of the Godhead is fully divine. Therefore, any of the Persons may be addressed in prayer. On this basis, prayer to the Holy Spirit is proper, even though Scripture does not speak explicitly of such prayer. Because the Three are one God, it is also proper to address prayer to the triune God, without making a distinction of persons in our minds. The usual pattern in the New Testament, however, is for prayer to be made to the Father, through the Son, with the help of the Holy Spirit. C. S. Lewis put it this way in his discussion of the Trinity:

> An ordinary simple Christian kneels down to say his prayers. He is trying to get in touch with God. But if he is a Christian he knows that what is prompting him to pray is God: God, so to speak, inside him. But he also knows that all his real knowledge of God comes through Christ, the Man who was God—that Christ is standing beside him, helping him to pray, praying for him....So

the whole threefold life of the three-personal God is actually going on in that ordinary little bedroom where an ordinary man is
saying his prayers. (*Mere Christianity*, p. 127)

Since prayer is ordinarily directed to the Father, it will be
profitable to consider further the significance of the use of "Father" as a form of address in prayer.

In the recorded prayers of Jesus, all but one have this form
of address. (The exception is the cry from the cross, recorded in
Matt. 27:46 and Mark 15:34.) Not only did Jesus address His
prayer to the Father, but He taught His disciples to do so as well.
This is clear in the giving of the Lord's Prayer (Matt. 6:6-15;
Luke 11:2-13) and also in the statements about prayer in the farewell discourse (John 15:16; 16:23). On the basis of this example
and instruction, the early church was in the habit of praying to
the Father (Eph. 1:17; 3:14; Col. 1:12; 3:17; 1 Pet. 1:17, etc.)
Even the Aramaic word that Jesus had used for Father, "*Abba,*"
the affectionate household word like "Daddy," persisted in the
prayers of Greek-speaking Christians (Rom. 8:15; Gal. 4:6).

An interesting but somewhat misleading interpretation of
the use of this title is offered by Joachim Jeremias (*The Prayers
of Jesus*, pp. 54-65). He asserts that there was no precedent in
the Old Testament for an *individual* to address God as Father.
This is not to say that the concept of God as Father was unknown, but that He was never addressed in that way in prayer.
To do so, Jeremias believes, is an innovation traceable directly
to Jesus Himself.

Jeremias does not interpret Jesus' use of the name Father
in a trinitarian way. Rather he understands it as expressing a
new understanding of God developed by Jesus. Jeremias thinks
that Jesus' uniqueness lay in the fullness of revelation that was
given Him by God, by which He realized the authority and kindness of God. He expressed that view of God by calling Him
"My Father."

This view of Jeremias does not do justice to all that the Scriptures teach. It is true that the name "Father" contains a reference to God's authority and benevolence. This is certainly the point of Jesus' analogy in Luke 11:11-13, in which an earthly father's love is used to give assurance of God's willingness to answer prayer. God's authority as Father is spoken of in Hebrews 12:7: "If you endure chastening, God deals with you as with sons; for what son is there whom a father does not chasten?" This is why the beginning of the Lord's Prayer has frequently been interpreted as an encouragement to come to God. As Calvin wrote:

> It is as if we addressed Him, "O Father, who dost abound with great devotion toward Thy children, and with great readiness to forgive, we Thy children call upon Thee...persuaded that Thou bearest toward us only the affection of a father, although we are unworthy of such a father." (*Institutes*, III:XX:37)

Beyond this, however, the use of the name "Father" in prayer often refers to a distinct Person of the Godhead. When Jesus prays to His Father in heaven, He is expressing a relationship with the Father that is unique. Jesus never joins with His disciples in praying to "*our* Father." He is praying as the eternal Son of God to His eternal Father, who is distinguished as a Person from Himself. This is clearly seen in His great high-priestly prayer: "And now, O Father, glorify Me together with Yourself, with the glory which I had with You before the world was" (John 17:5).

When believers use the name "Father" in prayer, then, it has a different meaning than when it is used by Jesus—but not totally so. For it denotes the same *Person* in both cases. In the New Testament, praying to the Father is not only praying to the God who acts toward us in a fatherly way, but also calling upon the Father as distinguished from the Son and the Spirit. Frequently the names of the Son and the Holy Spirit occur in the same contexts in which prayer to the Father is mentioned:

> I bow my knees to the Father of our Lord Jesus Christ...that He would grant you...to be strengthened with might through His Spirit in the inner man, that Christ may dwell in your hearts through faith. (Eph. 3:14-17)

> Do all in the name of the Lord Jesus, giving thanks to God the Father through Him. (Col. 3:17)

Even when the word "Father" is not used, "God" may refer to Him in distinction from the Son and Spirit (see Acts 4:24-28). In most cases, prayer in the New Testament is prayer to God the Father, the first Person of the Trinity.

Thus, while prayer to the Son or the Spirit is not improper, the normal pattern is for prayer to be addressed specifically to the Father as the one who hears and answers prayer. However, we should not divide the work of the Father from that of the Son and the Spirit, but be conscious that in the total experience of prayer the Father, Son, and Spirit are graciously working in perfect and unbroken unity.

Questions for Discussion and Reflection

⚘ Discuss the doctrine of providence (as defined in *Shorter Catechism* Q. 11), and explain how it relates to prayer.

⚘ Read Psalm 86, and list the expressions in it that speak of the nature of God.

⚘ Prayer to the "saints" is sometimes defended as being the same as asking living Christians to pray for us. How do you respond?

⚘ What does it mean to pray, as Jesus did, "Your will be done"?

⚘ State briefly the doctrine of the Trinity. Contrast the views of Paul Tillich and C. S. Lewis concerning the relation between the doctrine of the Trinity and prayer.

Chapter Four

The Role of Jesus Christ in Prayer

T he teaching of the Bible about the role that Jesus Christ performs in prayer may be divided into two categories. The Bible presents Him as the preeminent teacher about prayer. It also tells us that He is the only mediator between God and man in prayer.

Jesus as the Teacher of Prayer

Many of God's prophets and apostles have taught us about prayer in the Bible. Jesus' doctrine stands in continuity with the teaching of the Old Testament; and after Him Paul, James, John, Peter, and the writer of the Epistle to the Hebrews, add valuable instruction. But among all the teachers about prayer, He occupies the supreme position. The Bible records more teaching about prayer from Him than from anyone else. Here, too, no one ever spoke as this Man spoke. The Christian Church has based its understanding of prayer, and the practice of it, primarily on the teaching of Jesus. The Lord's Prayer has had a prominent place in the worship of the Church, and in all ages it has formed the basis for catechetical instruction and theological reflection on prayer. (Think of the questions and answers on the Lord's Prayer in the *Westminster Shorter Catechism*.) Jesus indicated that His own teaching was essential for the practice of prayer when He said, "If you abide in Me, *and My words abide in you* [italics added], you will ask what you desire, and it shall be done for you" (John 15:7). The content of Jesus' teaching on prayer forms the basis of a large part of this study on prayer, and will not be discussed in detail here.

The teaching of Jesus on prayer is not limited to His words. It was as they observed Jesus' practice of prayer that the disciples came to Him with the request, "Lord, teach us to pray" (Luke 11:1). The prayer life of Jesus, like other aspects of His life, was exemplary, and worthy of our imitation.

Often the Gospel writers record Jesus' practice of finding places where He might be alone to pray (Matt. 14:23; Luke 5:16; 9:18). He prayed before dawn (Mark 1:35), and on one occasion prayed all night (Luke 6:12). He prayed for others: for little children (Matt. 19:13), for Peter (Luke 22:32), for all who believe in Him (John 17). He often gave thanks (Matt. 11:25; 15:36; John 11:41-42). In times of great distress and suffering He had recourse to prayer: in Gethsemane (Matt. 26:26-36 and parallels) and on the cross (Matt. 27:46; Luke 23:34, 46).

Hebrews 5:7-8 speaks of the prayer experience of Jesus as one of the aspects of His identification with us in the struggles of human existence:

> In the days of His flesh, when He had offered up prayers and supplications, with vehement cries and tears to Him who was able to save Him from death, and was heard because of His godly fear...He learned obedience by the things which He suffered.

John Calvin says that this passage gives us practical instruction for prayer:

What better guidance can we have as to prayer than the example of Christ? He betook Himself immediately to the Father. And thus the Apostle indicates what ought to be done by us when he says that He offered prayers to Him that was able to deliver Him from death. (*Commentary on Hebrews*)

While only glimpses are given us of the prayer life of Jesus, what is given to us is full of instruction. Jesus, then, is the foremost teacher of prayer, whose instruction and example set a pattern for prayer that is valid in all times.

Jesus' Work as the Mediator for Prayer

The possibility of effective prayer depends upon the mediatorial work of Christ. Christian prayer is prayer to God *through* Jesus Christ. We now turn our attention to the many passages in which the connection between prayer and the activity of Christ is explained.

Prayer in the Name of Christ

The first set of passages connecting prayer with Christ is found in the Gospel of John. In His farewell discourse, Jesus spoke repeatedly of prayer *in His name*. He promised that whatever was asked in His name would be granted (John 14:13-14; 15:16). Not only that, but the answer also would be given in His name (John 16:23). Finally, He indicated that to ask in His name was something new, a privilege not before enjoyed by His followers (John 16:24). To these passages may be added Ephesians 5:20: "giving thanks always for all things to God the Father in the name of our Lord Jesus Christ."

A common understanding of the meaning of praying in Christ's name was expressed by F. Godet in the earlier editions of his *Commentary on the Gospel of John*:

To ask in the name of anyone is, in ordinary life, to ask in place of a person, as if on his part, and applying to oneself, in virtue of his recommendation, all his titles to the favour demanded. (vol. II, p. 227)

With this explanation, prayer in Christ's name would be prayer made on the basis of a right granted by Christ. While this understanding is in harmony with scriptural teaching, it does not do justice to Jesus' meaning in these passages, for He also speaks of the Father acting in Christ's name (John 14:26). Nowhere else in Scripture do we find that the Son grants authority to the Father; rather, authority flows to the incarnate Son of God from the Father.

A more satisfactory interpretation of the phrase "in My name," as Godet later realized, places emphasis upon the revelatory character of Jesus' name. To pray in His name is "to ask a thing of God as Father *on the foundation of the revelation* which Jesus has given us of Himself and of His work" (p. 277). The asking is within the boundaries of the revelation of the person and work of Christ, and takes the fullness of that revelation into account.

With this understanding, it becomes clear how the activity of the Father can be in the name of the Son. The Father sends the Holy Spirit in the name of Christ, that is, in connection with what is revealed concerning the work of redemption, in harmony with, and in fulfillment of that work of Christ. Also, the Father answers prayer in the name of Jesus, not because the Son has authorized Him to do so, but rather in connection with Christ's work of atonement and intercession. Answers to prayer are given within the circle of the revelation embodied in the name of the Lord Jesus Christ.

Other statements of Jesus become clear when His name is understood to refer to the fullness of revelation concerning His person and work. It is not strange to hear of prayer being made to *Jesus* in His own name (John 14:14), when that is understood to mean that the prayer must be in harmony with what is included in His name. And it becomes plain in what sense prayer in Christ's name is a new privilege (John 16:24). As Calvin notes, even in the Old Testament times "It was...one of the principles of faith, that prayers offered to God when there was no Mediator were rash and useless." Yet, believers then "did not clearly and fully understand what was meant" (*Commentary on....John*, on 16:24). That is, the *name* of Christ was not yet fully known. When the revelation was complete (the 'day' to which Jesus refers in John 16:23, 26 is the day of His resurrection, which would usher in a new era of spiritual privileges) then prayer would stand on a new level.

> From the time that Christ gave His life for His friends...and for their salvation sat down on the right hand of God...His name would become to them, in quite a new sense, the pledge and guarantee of their prayers being heard. (E. W. Hengstenberg, *Commentary on...John*, on 16:24)

Prayer in Christ's name, then, is much more than habitually ending our prayers with some mention of Him. It means responding in our whole being to the truth that comes to fullness of revelation in Him, participating in the new life that comes from Him, and submitting to His authority and teaching. (Of course, that fullness of revelation in Christ includes the understanding that as sinners we have no *right* to receive God's blessing, and that Christ has purchased blessing for us.)

Jesus as the High Priest of Prayer

The work of Jesus Christ for our salvation has often been described in terms of His offices of Prophet, Priest, and King. It is in His priestly office that Christ performs His distinctive work in relation to prayer. That work is most clearly described in the Book of Hebrews.

The priestly work of Christ is first connected with prayer in Hebrews 4:14-16:

> Seeing then that we have a great High Priest who has passed through the heavens, Jesus the Son of God...let us therefore come boldly to the throne of grace, that we may obtain mercy and find grace to help in time of need.

This passage makes use of the Oriental imagery of a subject approaching the king's throne room to ask a favor. We may think, for example, of Esther coming into the presence of King Ahasuerus to request the rescue of her people (Esther 5:1-4). Here it is clear that a heavenly throne is in view, and that the King who occupies it is God Himself (see Heb. 9:24). The purpose of approaching God is to obtain help. The drawing near is not a once-for-all act, not entrance into God's presence at death, for the verb is in the present tense. We keep coming to God for strength to face the trials and temptations of daily life, the constant pressure to abandon our profession of faith in Christ.

This approach to God is to be *with boldness*, that is, with openness, without shame or fear. (The contrast with Esther's situation is striking.) Of course, we must be aware of the danger of coming to God with a mistaken sense of our own worth, with a boldness that amounts to brashness. But the writer of Hebrews speaks here of a confidence whose basis has been explained in the preceding verses, resting entirely on the work of Christ on our behalf.

We may approach God with confidence because of the fact that believers have Jesus as their great high priest (v. 14). Hebrews 4:14-16 introduces the detailed discussion of Christ's priesthood, which occupies much of the remainder of the Epistle. This introductory statement emphasizes the sympathy with which Christ acts as our priest. This sympathy extends to the experience of prayer, for Jesus also prayed in the face of temptation (Heb. 5:7). Therefore, we can pray with confidence that in the very presence of the Father there is one who is able to enter fully into the needs that are being expressed. John Murray has finely stated what an encouragement this is to believers:

> And the thought that we in the stresses and conflicts associated with the body of our humiliation are objects of the solicitude and compassion of Him who sits at the right hand of the throne of

the majesty in the heavens and who dispenses from the reservoir of His knowledge and experience consolation, fellow-feeling, and strength injects into our fainting hearts the confidence of His invincible grace. (*The Heavenly Priestly Activity of Christ*, p. 9)

Another significant passage on prayer in Hebrews comes at the conclusion of the discussion of Christ's priestly work:

> Therefore, brethren, having boldness to enter the Holiest by the blood of Jesus, by a new and living way, which He consecrated for us, through the veil, that is, His flesh, and having a High Priest over the house of God, let us draw near with a true heart in full assurance of faith, having our hearts sprinkled from an evil conscience and our bodies washed with pure water. Let us hold fast the confession of our hope without wavering, for He who promised is faithful. (10:19-23)

The close parallelism between Hebrews 4:14-16 and 10:19-23 is apparent. Both passages contain exhortations to maintain our confession of Christ, and to draw near to God, on the basis of the fact that we possess Jesus as our high priest. Both speak of boldness or confidence as the manner in which a believer may approach God. The "drawing near" in both passages means prayer, even though chapter 10 does not mention the petitionary aspect of prayer.

In Hebrews 10:19, the place to which we come is "the Holiest," the sanctuary. In the ninth chapter of Hebrews, the heavenly sanctuary corresponds to the Holy of Holies in the Old Testament Tabernacle. As the high priest entered the innermost part of the Tabernacle once a year on the Day of Atonement (Heb. 9:7), so Christ has entered the heavenly sanctuary once for all:

> For Christ has not entered the holy places made with hands, which are copies of the true, but into heaven itself, now to appear in the presence of God for us. (Heb. 9:24)

The "sanctuary" is thus identified with the presence of God. Hebrews 10:19 speaks of access into the presence of God, the privilege that believers have of approaching God in prayer. This is equivalent to approaching the *throne* of grace, because Christ our high priest is "seated at the right hand of the throne of the majesty in the heavens" (Heb. 8:1).

Believers have "boldness to enter the Holiest by the blood of Jesus" (Heb. 10:19). The blood of Jesus is the means by which entrance into God's presence is possible. This statement refers back to Hebrews 9:12, where it was said that Christ's entrance into the sanctuary was *through His blood*. Why should it be said that Christ, the Son of God, who was without sin (Heb. 4:15), was barred from the presence of God, gaining admittance only through His blood? The answer lies in the priestly work of Christ, which is unfolded in this epistle.

As high priest, Jesus Christ identifies Himself with His people (Heb. 2:9-18). Because of this solidarity with sinners, Christ could not appear in the presence of God as their representative unless He dealt with their sin; and sin cannot be forgiven apart from the shedding of blood, that is, without the death of a sacrifice (Heb. 9:22). The blood of animal sacrifices only served for ceremonial cleansing, not for the cleansing of the conscience before God (Heb. 9:13; 10:4). Hence, the blood spilled by Jesus when He died on the cross represented the real sacrifice, a sacrifice that effectively removes the guilt of sin: "but now, once at the end of the ages, He has appeared to put away sin by the sacrifice of Himself" (Heb. 9:26). Because He has thus offered His life as a satisfaction of divine justice for the sins of His people, He is able to appear in the presence of God on their behalf (Heb. 9:24).

Not only does Jesus Christ stand in God's presence representing His people, He is the "forerunner" in whose steps believers are to follow (Heb. 6:20; 12:1-2). The entrance He has made possible by His sacrificial death is a way *for us* (Heb. 10:20), a way that believers may travel. Because of our union with our great high priest, and on the basis of the satisfaction for their sins that He has made, we are now able to follow Him into the presence of God, as we pray. As Franz Delitzsch has said,

> Christ, in high-priestly wise, has preceded us...we follow Him along the way which He has opened and formed for us, knowing ourselves to be now reconciled and sanctified by the one oblation...of His blood outpoured on earth and presented in heaven. (*Commentary on Hebrews*)

A further description is given in Hebrews 10:20 of the way of access to God: it is *new*. The term that is used originally meant "recently killed," but in later usage had the more general meaning of "new" or "fresh." This does not mean that access to the presence of God was unavailable before Christ came. Believers in the Old Testament enjoyed intimate fellowship with God, had their prayers answered and their sins forgiven, as many of the Psalms indicate. This is not because they had another way of coming to God than through Christ. Rather, the death of Christ, as foreordained by God and therefore certain, was effective for the forgiveness of the sins of God's true people even before it actually occurred in history. The blood that Jesus shed was "the blood of the everlasting covenant" (Heb. 13:20), efficacious in all ages (see Rev. 13:8). Hence the term "new" means that the way to God is more clearly seen and understood by believers since Christ came. The "way into the Holiest of All was not yet made manifest while the first tabernacle was still standing." (Heb. 9:8) The way is not absolutely, but relatively new, in terms of the fuller understanding and assurance possessed by believers under the New Covenant. As Delitzsch says:

> No saint of the Old Testament, in whatever degree he might stand of preparatory or prevenient grace, could...draw nigh to God so confidently, so joyously, so familiarly, as we can now. (*Commentary on Hebrews*)

The way of access is also described as *living* (Heb. 10:20). This cannot merely mean "effective," as if it were in contrast to the deadness of the Old Testament way of access, for believers in that time did have access to God, as has just been shown. Rather, this expression points to the fact that access to God involves a vital personal union with Christ. Coming to God involves more than an intellectual understanding that propitiation for sin has been made; it requires entering into a relationship with the High Priest who is a living Person, indeed, one who is "alive forevermore" (Rev. 1:18).

The words "through the veil, that is, His flesh" (Heb. 10:20) have a two-fold meaning. They point to the Day of Atonement, when the high priest passed through the veil into the Holy of Holies. They also refer to the "flesh"; the genuine humanity of Jesus. It may be that the bodily suffering of Christ was difficult to accept for the Hebrew Christians to whom this letter was written, so that it was necessary to stress that entrance into God's presence was only by means of that suffering. Calvin has captured the sense of the symbolism well, when he says that the flesh of Christ "conceals as a veil the majesty of God, while it is also that which conducts us to the enjoyment of all the good things of God" (*Commentary*). Both the objective right to enter God's presence, and the subjective assurance of that right, depend upon the historical reality that "the Word became flesh and dwelt among us" (John 1:14), and that He was "put to death in the flesh" (1 Pet. 3:18).

One other reason is given for the exhortation to draw near to God in prayer: "having a High Priest over the house of God" (Heb. 10:21). The priestly work of Christ continues. The verb for this verse is supplied from verse 19: *having*. The offering of the sacrifice was once for all, not to be repeated (Heb. 9:25-26). Now Christ continues to serve as a high priest over the house of God (the Church), by (1) the exhibition of His blood, symbolically, as the basis on which believers are accepted and blessed by God (Heb. 9:12); (2) intercession for His own (Heb. 7:25);

and (3) the actual granting of aid to those who are in need (Heb. 2:18).

We have already shown how prayer depends on the blood, that is, the sacrifice of Christ. Calvin regards the continuing efficacy of Christ's sacrifice as the essence of His intercession:

> But the value of His sacrifice, by which He once pacified God toward us, is always powerful and efficacious; the blood by which He atoned for our sins, the obedience which He rendered, is a continual intercession for us. (*Commentary*)

However, Christ's intercession involves more than obtaining the removal of guilt for sin. In Hebrews 7:25, the continuing intercession of Christ is said to provide salvation "to the uttermost" — salvation in its fullness. In Romans 8:34, the intercession of Christ is presented as the basis of the believer's assurance that all the assaults of adversaries will not be able to rob believers of the eternal enjoyment of the love of God. When we add to these statements the fact that Jesus during His earthly ministry prayed for specific blessings for those who believed in Him (Luke 23:34; John 17), it is clear that the priestly work of Christ involves petition for us. As John Murray has said:

> The intercession covers the whole range of what is requisite to, and of what is realized in the eschatological salvation....No grace bestowed, no blessing enjoyed, no benefit received can be removed from the scope of the intercession. (*The Heavenly, Priestly Activity of Christ*, p. 55)

Is there a relationship between the fact that Christ prays for us, and our own praying? Hebrews 10:20-21 teaches that there is. Because Christ continues to make intercession for us, we may draw near to God in prayer. Our desire to pray, our knowledge of what to pray for, and our confidence to come to God, are gifts of God, given in answer to Christ's prayer to the Father. In so far as we pray according to God's will, we enjoy the confidence that our prayers are joined to those of our great High Priest, whose intercession is always availing.

The third aspect of Christ's continuing priesthood, that of granting aid, serves as an encouragement to prayer in that Christ, as a sympathetic High Priest, is united with the Father in His throne, and, with the Father, sends the Spirit and answers prayer (John 16:7; 14:14). In this way Christ acts as a King as well as Priest, "according to the order of Melchizedek" (Heb. 5:10).

Prayer occupies a prominent place in the teaching of Jesus, but He is more than a teacher of prayer. His teaching cannot be separated from who He is and what He has done. By means of His obedience, suffering, and death He has removed the barrier of sin, so that those who believe in Him are now reconciled to God. Prayer is one of the privileges of the new relationship between God and the redeemed. Prayer also depends on the continuing priesthood of Christ, in which He pleads the efficacy of His sacrifice, makes intercession for His own, and powerfully helps and provides for them. One who prays in His Name takes into account all of His teaching, keeping within its bounds, and rests upon the Savior's work in all its aspects. Only by praying in that way can we be confident that our praying will be acceptable to God. True prayer rests upon Christ's own words: "I am the way, the truth, and the life. No one comes to the Father except through Me" (John 14:6).

Questions for Discussion and Reflection

✗ What features of the example of Jesus Christ in prayer are most challenging and helpful to you?

✗ What has been your understanding of what it means to pray in the name of Christ? Did the chapter give you any new insights?

✗ Read Hebrews 4:14-16, and see if you can make a list of ten lessons about prayer that you learn from this text.

✗ According to Hebrews 10:19-23, what is the connection between the death of Christ and our ability to come to God in prayer?

✗ What is the nature of Christ's intercession for us, and how does it affect our praying?

Chapter Five
The Work of the Holy Spirit in Prayer

The possibility and efficacy of prayer rest not only on the work of Christ, through whom we have access to God, but also on the work of the Holy Spirit. The Apostle Paul, having asserted that Gentiles who were separated from God "have been brought near by the blood of Christ" (Eph. 2:13), adds that "through Him we both have access by one Spirit to the Father" (Eph. 2:18). Christians are to be filled with the Spirit, and that filling will be shown in praise and giving of thanks (Eph. 6:18).

Obviously, prayer cannot be fully understood apart from an understanding of the Spirit's work in it. There are two aspects of the Spirit's work in prayer: He provides motivation and guidance for our praying, and He makes intercession for us.

The Spirit's Motivation and Guidance in Prayer

In two closely related passages, Paul shows how prayer is the result of the Spirit's presence in the life of the believer. The first is Romans 8:15: "For you did not receive the spirit of bondage again to fear, but you received the Spirit of adoption by whom we cry out, 'Abba! Father!'" The parallel passage is Galatians 4:6: "And because you are sons, God has sent forth the Spirit of His Son into your hearts, crying out, 'Abba, Father!'" The two passages help to explain each other, and should be studied together.

The first fact to be noted is that both of these verses refer to the Holy Spirit. Some translations have "spirit of adoption" (with a small "s") in Romans 8:15, but the fact that it is clearly the Holy Spirit who is referred to in Romans 8:14, 16, along with the obvious similarity of the two verses, indicates that the Holy Spirit is referred to in Romans 8:15 as well. The Spirit has been sent by the Father (Gal. 4:6; see John 14:26), and believers have received Him (Rom. 8: 15).

As a result of receiving the Spirit, the believer cries "Abba!" In Galatians 4:6 it is the Spirit who cries; in Romans 8:15, believers cry. The connection between these two statements is indicated by the "by whom" of Romans 8:15. When Christians cry out "Abba!" it is the result of the Spirit's assurance that they are children of God. The cry can be attributed to both the Spirit, and to the one who prays, without any contradiction. The relationship between the Spirit and the one who prays is not merely complementary, as though each had an equal part. All of our work is done only because God motivates and enables us (see Phil. 2:12-13). Our crying is at the same time the Spirit's crying within us.

The cry "Abba!" in both passages signifies the status of sonship that believers enjoy since the coming of Christ, in contrast to the status as servants that characterized believers under the old covenant (Gal. 4:7). The title "Spirit of adoption" is given Him "because it is He who creates in the children of God the filial love and confidence by which they are able to cry 'Abba Father' and enjoy the rights and privileges of God's children" (John Murray, *Romans*, p. 296). "Abba" is a deeply significant word. It is Aramaic, and thus it is surprising that Paul should use it in writing to Greek-speaking people in Rome and Galatia. The reason seems to be that this was the word that Jesus used to address His Father in prayer, as Mark specifically tells us (14:36). "Abba" would have been the word the Savior used when He gave the Lord's Prayer to His disciples. Thus Paul could use this foreign word in writing these epistles, because his readers would have known of its use by Jesus.

It is not simply our *consciousness* that God is our Father, but our *ability to pray* to Him as Father, which the Apostle here attributes to the Spirit. The verb that is used denotes loud crying of any kind, but is commonly used in the Septuagint, especially in the Psalms, of prayer to God. Jesus' prayer is described in a similar way in Hebrews 5:7. The loudness of the cry may well express the confidence with which it is uttered:

> In calling is expressed the certainty and joy with which one who is moved by the Spirit turns to God. The address of servants, on the other hand, is the murmured prayer prescribed by Jewish custom. (*TDNT*, III, pp. 898ff)

The teaching of Romans 8:15 and Galatians 4:6, then, is that our ability and inclination to pray comes from the Holy Spirit who dwells within us. The Spirit makes us aware of our status as children of God, and opens our eyes to the inheritance to which we now have a claim (Rom 8:16-17). The cry of "Abba!" must include praise and adoration and thanksgiving to the One who has made such guilty and undeserving sinners His children. It includes the submission that is appropriate on the part of a son to his father. And it surely involves requests to the Father for the blessings that are now ours, and of which we stand in need, including the forgiveness of our sins. (The Prodigal

Son is our model here.) The cry "Abba! Father!" contains every aspect of prayer.

Other passages expand our knowledge of the Holy Spirit's ministry in prayer. If we are to pray aright, we must be aware of our real needs, and we must know that the resources to meet those needs are to be found in God alone. It is the Holy Spirit who convinces of sin (John 16:8), and He opens our eyes to see the grace of God that is proclaimed in the Gospel (1 Cor. 2:9-12). Apart from His work, we would neither honor God nor give thanks (Rom. 1:21). Prayers of praise and thanksgiving are impossible unless the Spirit is at work (Eph. 5:18-20). Praying for others requires love, which is a fruit of the Spirit (Gal. 5:22). There is no element of true prayer that cannot be traced back to the operation of the Holy Spirit in the life of a believer.

The Holy Spirit's Intercession

We now turn to a passage that speaks most directly of the Spirit's work in prayer:

> Likewise the Spirit also helps in our weaknesses. For we do not know what we should pray for as we ought, but the Spirit Himself makes intercession for us with groanings which cannot be uttered. Now He who searches the hearts knows what the mind of the Spirit is, because He makes intercession for the saints according to the will of God. (Rom. 8:26-27)

This passage refers to assistance given by the Holy Spirit in prayer because of our infirmity. He remedies our weakness by His intercession.

There have been two views among Reformed scholars about this intercession of the Spirit. Some have held, with Calvin, that it refers to the teaching ministry of the Spirit, who corrects our ignorance of what to pray for by instructing us. As Calvin expresses it, "we are taught by the same Spirit how to pray, and what to ask for in our prayers" (*Commentary on Romans*, p. 312).

Abraham Kuyper, on the other hand, views the intercession of
the Spirit as an activity wholly distinct from the believer's own
efforts in prayer:

> But being unable of ourselves to kindle the incense, the Holy
> Spirit helps our infirmities, and from our hearts prays to God in
> our behalf. We are not conscious of it; He prays for and in us with
> groans that cannot be uttered; which does not mean that He makes
> us utter groans for which we cannot account, but that He groans
> in us. (*The Work of the Holy Spirit*, p. 639)

The question, then, is whether this text refers to the Spirit's
enabling believers to pray, or to His prayer for them.

There are several reasons why it is best to understand this
verse as referring to an activity of the Holy Spirit that is distinct
from our own praying:

⟩ℴ The phrase "the Spirit Himself" places an emphasis upon
   the fact that the Spirit is the one who is acting. A distinction
   from the human spirit seems to be implied (see Rom. 8:16).

⟩ℴ The verb translated "makes intercession" means "to appeal
   or petition," and it is accompanied by a preposition that
   means "for the benefit of another." The general idea of "helping," i.e., by instructing the believer in what to pray for,
   does not fit the words that are used.

⟩ℴ The Spirit's intercession is said to take place in "unuttered"
   (or "unutterable") groanings. As in Romans 8:23, there is
   an expression here of deep desire and longing. These desires are not spoken in an articulate way, and therefore it
   seems that the Spirit's intercession does not result in vocal
   prayer. If the Spirit's work in this text were *instruction* in the
   proper content of prayer, the outcome would be the expression of that content once it was grasped by the mind.

These factors justify the conclusion that Romans 8:26-27 is
describing a work of the Holy Spirit in believers in which, apart
from their conscious willing or understanding, He asks the Fa-

ther for those benefits that they need. And we have the assurance that this intercession is effective. When verse 27 says that "He who searches the hearts knows what the mind of the Spirit is," that would mean very little if "knows" means only "is aware of." When it is added, "because He makes intercession for the saints according to the will of God," then it is clear that this verse teaches that the Father *recognizes and approves* what the Spirit asks. The Father grants what the Spirit requests, because it is in agreement with His nature and purpose.

It is difficult to tell whether or not these verses teach that we are consciously aware of the Spirit's intercession. It is clear, however, that the intercession takes place in the heart, for it is as the one who "searches the hearts" that the Father takes notice of it. Kuyper holds that the believer is entirely unconscious of the Spirit's pleading (*Work of the Holy Spirit*, p. 639). On the other hand, the Spirit is not *located* (in a spatial sense) in believers. He dwells in our hearts in the sense that He is graciously and powerfully at work in the very center of our being. Therefore, it seems that in some way the groaning must be attributed to us as well as to the Spirit. It does not *begin* from our own understanding and will, but it is from our hearts; it cannot be separated from the new life given us by the indwelling Spirit. John Murray's summary captures the thought of this passage well:

> As God searches the heart of the children of God He finds unuttered and unutterable groanings. Though they are thus inarticulate, there is a meaning and intent that cannot escape the omniscient eye of God—they are wholly intelligible to Him. And, furthermore, they are found to be in accordance with His will...because, though surpassing our understanding and utterance, they are indited by the Holy Spirit and are the ways in which His intercessions come to expression in our consciousness. (*Romans*, I, p. 313)

Although this particular text does not teach that the Holy Spirit instructs our minds in the proper content of prayer, what was said earlier in the study of Romans 8:15 and Galatians 4:6 should be remembered. As Christians, we do possess the ability to pray, and that ability is given us by the Holy Spirit. The Spirit's instruction in prayer and His intercession go together. As Abraham Kuyper wrote:

> Apart from the intercession in our behalf there is also a work of His Person *in our own prayers*....The Holy Spirit prays in us as long and in as much as we can not pray for ourselves; but at the same time He teaches *us* to pray, that gradually His prayer may become superfluous. (*Work of the Holy Spirit*, p. 639)

The work of the Holy Spirit is the prerequisite for every aspect of prayer. Therefore, it is a continuation of the discussion of His work in prayer as we turn now to consider prayer in its subjective aspects. We will consider the qualifications that are produced in us by the Spirit to enable us to pray; and then the content of proper prayer as guided by the same Spirit.

Questions for Discussion and Reflection

❧ What are several English equivalents of the word "Abba" when used in prayer? What does this word teach us about prayer?

❧ What is the connection between our praying to God as "Abba" and the work of the Holy Spirit?

❧ What are the two main views concerning the Spirit's intercession (Rom. 8:26)?

❧ What encouraging truth(s) about prayer did you learn from this chapter?

Chapter Six
Qualifications
in the One Who Prays

P rayer, according to the Bible, involves a personal relationship between God and the one who is praying. In
prayer, we are not manipulating or invoking some
unknown Power, but calling upon the living God. True prayer
regards God as a Person, who hears and reacts to prayer. Fur-
thermore, the one who prays is not a robot, but a person who is
involved in communication with God. Therefore, the form and
words of a prayer are important only as they are the genuine
expression of the thoughts and desires of a person. That this is
the case appears from the emphasis in the Bible upon the personal state of the one who would pray aright. According to
Scripture, the person who prays must be reverent, submissive,
sincere, believing, and obedient.

Reverence
The Old Testament emphasizes the need for reverence in
approaching God. The regulations of the ceremonial law and

the striking acts of judgment when men dealt carelessly with holy things (Lev. 10:1-3; 1 Chron. 13:5-10, etc.) served to impress upon God's people His holiness and transcendence. There is warning about irreverence in prayer:

> Walk prudently when you go to the house of God; and draw near to hear rather than to give the sacrifce of fools....
> Do not be rash with your mouth,
> And let not your heart utter anything hastily before God.
> For God is in heaven, and you on earth;
> Therefore let your words be few. (Eccl. 5:1-2)

When Jesus taught His disciples to use a child's word for Father, "Abba," in speaking to God, He was not repudiating the need for reverence in prayer. In the Lord's Prayer, there is a qualification; God is to be addressed as "Our Father in heaven" (Matt. 6:9). As Calvin indicates, these words are not meant to "locate" God, as though He were in heaven and, therefore, not on earth. But, "it is as if He had been said to be of infinite greatness or loftiness, or incomprehensible essence, of boundless might, and of everlasting immortality." (*Institutes*, III:XX:40) Even in approaching God as Father, we are to be aware of the distance that separates His divinity from our humanity. And so the petition follows, "Hallowed be Your name" (Matt. 6:9). That is:

> Help us first of all to know Thee rightly, and to hallow, glorify and praise Thee in all Thy works through which there shine almighty power, wisdom, goodness, righteousness, mercy, and truth. (*Heidelberg Catechism*, Q. 22)

Reflection on the majesty, power, and purity of God leads to a reverent attitude in prayer.

Sincerity

Jesus' rebuke of the Jewish religious leaders of his day included a denunciation of their hypocrisy in prayer. "And when you pray, you shall not be like the hypocrites. For they love to pray standing in the synagogues and on the corners of the streets, that they may be seen by men. Assuredly, I say to you, they have their reward." (Matt. 6:5). "Beware of the scribes, who...for a pretense make long prayers" (Mark 12:38, 40). Behind such hypocrisy lay the self-satisfaction of such leaders. Their prayers were unreal because they had no sense of their own need, and therefore no real desire for the grace of God.

The Scriptures not only condemn hypocritical prayer, but speak positively of the need for sincerity in prayer. Jesus warned against the heaping up of empty phrases in prayer (Matt. 6:7–8); yet in two of His parables He encouraged persistence in prayer when an answer is delayed (Luke 11:5-8; 18:1-7). He certainly did not mean that by mere mechanical repetition God's resistance is broken down. The force of these parables is obviously in an implied contrast between the sleepy friend and the unjust judge on the one hand, and God on the other. Persistent prayer reflects faith that is not vanquished by lack of immediate results (see Matt. 15:22-28); but it also implies fervent desire, an unwillingness to be satisfied unless the request is granted. Descriptions of exemplary instances of prayer often include the fact that such prayers were made with earnestness. The publican who prayed for mercy "beat his breast" as an indication of the strength of his emotion (Luke 18:13). Christ's prayers were made with "vehement cries and tears" (Heb. 5:7); in Gethsemane He prayed "more earnestly" (Luke 22:44). When Peter was imprisoned, "constant" prayer was made for him by the church (Acts 12:5). Elijah is said to have prayed "earnestly" (Jas. 5:17).

Calvin makes it one of the basic rules of prayer:

...that in our petitions we ever sense our own insufficiency, and earnestly pondering how we need all that we seek, join with this prayer an earnest—nay, burning—desire to attain it....Now what do we account more hateful...to God than the fiction of someone asking pardon for his sins, all the while either thinking he is not a sinner, or at least not thinking he is a sinner? (*Institutes*, III:XX:6)

Submission

Fervent desire, of course, does not stand by itself as a requirement for prayer. The sovereignty of God demands that human desire be submissive to His will.

The foremost example of submissive prayer is that of Jesus in Gethsemane: "My Father, if it is possible, let this cup pass from Me; nevertheless, not as I will, but as You will" (Matt. 26:39). The believer, if he prays sincerely, manifests a similar attitude when he prays, "Your will be done on earth as it is in heaven" (Matt. 6:10). In asking this, Calvin says:

> We renounce the desires of our flesh; for whoever does not resign and submit his feelings to God opposes as much as he can God's will, since only what is corrupt comes forth from us. (*Institutes*, III:XX:43)

Paul's experience in prayer indicates how submission places bounds upon importunity in prayer. He prayed three times for the removal of his thorn; but when it was revealed to him that it was not God's will to remove it, he gladly submitted to the will of the Father (2 Cor. 12:8-9).

This attitude of submission in prayer does not remain merely a kind of restraint, in that one does not insist on his own will as ultimate. But, in so far as the will of God is revealed, and hence is known, submission involves embracing that will, and desiring that it be done. Submission to God's will determines in a positive way the content of prayer. Prayer made in submission to God thus comes to be prayer "according to His will" (1 John 5:14).

Faith

Scripture clearly indicates that faith is an essential condition for efficacious prayer. Jesus stated this positively when He said, "And whatever things you ask in prayer, believing, you will receive" (Matt. 21:22). The condition is stated negatively by James, when he says concerning the man praying for wisdom:

> But let him ask in faith, nothing doubting; for he that doubteth is like the surge of the sea driven by the wind and tossed. For let not that man think that he shall receive anything of the Lord. (Jas. 1:6-7 ARV)

The content of faith is not stated in these two passages. But their contexts, and other passages in which faith in relation to prayer is discussed, show that this faith does have a definite content. "The prayer of faith" (Jas. 5:15) is prayer that involves the conviction that certain things are true, that a certain state of affairs actually exists.

Much of the preceding discussion has dealt with the objective facts that make prayer possible. It has been necessary, all along, to speak of the faith-content that is implicit in true prayer. What remains to be done here is to show that when faith is mentioned in Scripture as a condition of prayer, it means believing that these facts as true. It will be seen that faith involves an inward conviction of the truth of God's existence, power, and benevolence; and, in connection with the latter, of the efficacy of Christ's redemptive work.

Belief in the Existence of God

That prayer involves belief in the existence of a Hearer of prayer might seem so obvious as not to require statement. However, the existence of an altar to an unknown god, to which Paul refers (Acts 17:23), points to the possibility of prayer as a "shot in the dark," made on the chance that such a prayer might be heard and answered. And there are contemporary attempts to maintain prayer in the absence of belief in a personal God capable of hearing prayer. Hence, it is not without reason that the writer of Hebrews says that "without faith it is impossible to please Him. For whoever would draw near to God must believe that He is" (Heb. 11:6). Paul indicates that the faith that is essential for prayer is belief in God when he asks, "How then shall they call on Him in whom they have not believed? And how shall they believe in Him of whom they have not heard?" (Rom. 10:14). Faith here is clearly understood to be a believing acceptance of the revelation about God that He Himself has given.

Belief in the Power of God

A number of passages emphasize the fact that faith involves awareness of, and confidence in, God's unlimited power. In Hebrews, the God whose existence is believed is the God who created the world by His word of power (Heb. 11:3).

On a number of occasions Jesus taught that faith is a belief in God's omnipotence. He noted the greatness of the faith of the centurion, who was confident that simply by speaking a word of command, Jesus was able to heal his servant (Matt. 8:8-10). Jesus asked the blind men who sought healing, "Do you believe that I am able to do this?" Upon their affirmative reply, He said, "According to your faith let it be to you" (Matt. 9:27–29). The father of the epileptic boy was unsure whether Jesus was able to help or not; Jesus indicated that he lacked faith (Mark 9:17–24).

In these incidents, faith is seen to be confidence that nothing is beyond the power of the one in whom it is placed. The faith necessary for prayer is the kind of faith exemplified by Abraham:

> He did not waver at the promise of God through unbelief, but was strengthened in faith, giving glory to God, and being fully convinced that what He had promised He was also able to perform. (Rom. 4:20-21)

Belief in God's Benevolence

A number of passages point to God's willingness to grant help as the content of faith. Hebrews 11:6 says that beyond faith in God's existence, there is necessary for prayer the persuasion that He is the "rewarder" of those who seek Him. In James 1:5-6 the statement that prayer must be made in faith is preceded by the assertion that God "gives to all liberally and without reproach." Jesus declared that the faith of the Canaanite woman was great (Matt. 15:22-28). Her faith was manifested in the fact that she continued to ask for mercy in the face of an apparent rebuff; her importunity rested upon an unshakable conviction of the Savior's mercy.

Faith in God's benevolence does not exist in isolation from an awareness of His holiness, and of one's own sinfulness. Faith also takes into account the fact that "the wrath of God is revealed from heaven against all ungodliness and unrighteousness of men" (Rom. 1:18). Therefore, genuine faith in God's benevolence is necessarily faith in Jesus Christ, who has removed the barrier of sin between God and the redeemed by His obedience and sacrifice. The faith that is essential for prayer is faith in His finished work; in Him "we have boldness and access with confidence through faith in Him" (Eph. 3:12). The believer depends for God's acceptance of his prayer upon all that has been revealed concerning the high priestly work of Christ.

When faith refers to a belief in the revelation concerning the nature of God and the work of Jesus Christ, it is easy to see why doubt makes prayer ineffective. To doubt God's existence, or power, or benevolence, is to deny God Himself. It is an insult to His Name to regard anything as too hard for Him (see Jer. 32:17, 27). To think of Him as unwilling to help is to imply that evil men, who respond to the pleas of their children, are better than God (Matt. 7:9-11). The Epistle to the Hebrews, which develops so fully the doctrine of the priesthood of Christ as the basis for confidence in approaching God, also has very solemn warnings about the sin of unbelief, of spurning the Son of God (see Heb. 10:23, 26-31).

Doubt about the nature of God as the Hearer of prayer, and the redemption accomplished by Christ, is not weakness of faith, but the lack of it, and is culpable in the sight of God. Prayer without such faith does not please God (Heb. 11:6), and no answer to it is to be expected.

In Mark 11:22-24, faith in prayer is said to refer not only to the nature of God, but to the certainty that what is asked in prayer will actually be granted. The questions that arise concerning the ground for faith in this sense are so important that it will be best to discuss them separately in Chapter 7, on the content of prayer.

Obedience

There are a number of passages in which the efficacy of prayer is said to depend upon the "works" of the one who prays. Frequently in the Psalms the righteousness of the petitioner is given as a reason why his prayer should be heard: "Vindicate me, O Lord, / For I have walked in my integrity" (Ps. 26:1).

This cannot be dismissed as a sample of Old Testament "legalism." Jesus singled out one petition of the Lord's Prayer for comment:

> For if you forgive men their trespasses, your heavenly Father also will forgive you; but if you do not forgive men their trespasses, neither will your Father forgive your trespasses. (Matt. 6:14-15; see Mark 11:25; Matt. 18:23-35)

Here, one's willingness to forgive others is a condition for an answer to the prayer for forgiveness. A similar condition is stated in 1 John 3:22: "And whatever we ask we receive from Him, because we keep His commandments and do those things that are pleasing in His sight."

It might be concluded from these verses that answered prayer is a reward for the performance of acts of obedience. Upon closer examination, however, it is found that this is not the case. The context of 1 John 3:22 makes plain the relationship between obedience to God's commands and answered prayer. John has been discussing the command to love one another (1 John 3:11). But such love is not the means of gaining God's favor, but the evidence that one already has received spiritual life from God: "We know that we have passed from death to life, because we love the brethren" (1 John 3:14). Obedience of the command to love is a result of union with Christ: "Now he who keeps His commandments abides in Him, and He in him" (1 John 3:24). And only those who are thus united to Christ actually possess access to God, and therefore can pray with assurance that God will answer.

Obedience to the commands of God and willingness to forgive others are products, not causes, of salvation. They are evidences of regeneration, by which believers gain the right to call upon God as Father (see John 1:12-13). When the saints mention their own righteousness in prayer, Calvin says,

> By such expressions they mean nothing else but that by their regeneration itself they are attested as servants and children of God to whom He promises that He will be gracious. (*Institutes*, III:XX:10)

Thus it is appropriate to speak of obedience as a condition of prayer when obedience is understood as evidence that one has been given new life through faith in Christ. Only the truly converted can pray efficaciously.

Just as repentance is inseparable from union with Christ, so all the subjective conditions for prayer must be viewed as gifts that Christ imparts to those who are His own. Those who are in Christ Jesus are the sons of God through faith (Gal. 3:26); to those who are His children by virtue of their union with the Son, God has sent the Spirit of His Son, crying "Abba! Father!" (Gal. 4:6). And the Spirit works in them reverence, sincerity, submission, faith, obedience. These are not, therefore, conditions that are to be met by merely human effort, but are conditions that God Himself graciously works in those who receive and rest upon Jesus Christ alone for their salvation.

Questions for Discussion and Reflection

🜉 How do you resolve the tension between praying to God as a child to a father, and the need for reverence in prayer?

🜉 Explain the connection between sincerity and persistence in prayer.

🜉 Does it indicate a lack of faith when one prays "If it is your will"? Explain.

🜉 In Jesus' prayer in Gethsemane, was submission to the Father's will active or passive?

🜉 This chapter presents the conviction that the faith that is necessary for effective prayer has content, that it means believing certain things are true. Have you heard or read teaching about "the prayer of faith" that differs from this?

🜉 Does Matthew 6:14-15 mean that we must earn the right to have our prayers answered? Explain.

Chapter Seven

The Content of Prayer

The practice of prayer recorded in Scripture, and the commands regarding it, indicate that while it is proper to use the forms of prayer given by inspiration, the content of prayer need not be limited to these. The apostolic church continued to use the psalms in its worship (see Eph. 5:19); but prayer was not limited to these, nor to the actual form of the Lord's Prayer. There are many prayers that refer to specific historic situations: for example, the church's prayer for Peter when he was imprisoned (Acts 12:5), or Paul's prayer to be permitted to visit Rome (Rom. 1:9-10). The command, "Be anxious for nothing, but in everything by prayer and supplication, with thanksgiving, let your requests be made known to God" (Phil. 4:6), indicates that the specific causes of anxiety in a person's life are to be made matters of prayer. Therefore, prayer should not be limited to the use of fixed forms, even those given by inspiration.

Because the content of prayer is not restricted to the repetition of given forms, it must not be thought that there are no limits placed upon what may properly be asked of God in prayer. It is true that some statements of Scripture seem at first glance to promise that God will answer *whatever* request is made to Him. Jesus said:

> Ask, and it will be given to you; seek, and you will find; knock, and it will be opened to you. For every one who asks receives, and he who seeks finds, and to him who knocks it will be opened. (Matt. 7:7-8)

However, such a statement must not be separated from its context, nor from the teaching of Scripture as a whole. It must be interpreted along with the Lord's Prayer, which is a part of the same discourse of Jesus. Whenever the promise is made that "anything" asked in prayer will be granted, the "anything" is qualified in one way or another. God will grant "anything" that is asked in faith, or in the name of Christ, or in accordance with His will. By considering the significance of these qualifying statements, the content of proper prayer will be made clear.

The Prayer of Faith

The most significant passage in which faith appears as the condition of answered prayer is Mark 11:22-24:

> So Jesus answered and said to them, "Have faith in God. For assuredly, I say to you, whoever says to this mountain, 'Be removed and be cast into the sea,' and does not doubt in his heart, but believes that those things he says will be done, he will have whatever he says. Therefore I say to you, whatever things you ask when you pray, believe that you receive *them*, and you will have *them*." (see Matt. 21:21-22)

By these words, Jesus indicated that results no less amazing than the immediate withering of the barren fig tree would be granted to prayer that is made in faith.

The content of prayer to which an answer is promised is left indefinite: literally, "all things, as many as you pray" (Mark 11:24). The condition for the granting of prayer is believing that you receive. Lenski translates, "go on believing that you did receive them" (*Interpretation of St. Mark's Gospel*, p. 495). Faith in this case means a confident expectation that what is asked will be granted, a certainty that does not waver.

The question immediately arises as to the basis for such confidence. The context makes it clear that the faith spoken of in Mark 11:24 is not sheer credulity, not a "leap in the dark," but has its ground in what is objectively true. "Believe that you receive" in verse 24 must be taken with the "have faith in God" of verse 22. Faith that prayer will be answered is inseparable from faith in the God who answers prayer. Such faith, as has already been discussed, involves belief in God's ability and willingness to answer prayer. But it involves more: it is confidence also in the wisdom and the promise of God. One may believe in God's power and benevolence, and yet not be certain that a particular request will be granted, because he does not know whether it is according to God's will. Therefore, the "faith in God" that makes it possible "to believe that you receive" is faith in God's promise, in the revelation that He has made of His will.

Jesus gives a specific example to show that the faith that expects an answer to prayer rests upon God's word of promise and command: the mountain being cast into the sea (Mark 11:23). There is evidence that "moving a mountain" was a common metaphor for accomplishing the seemingly impossible. When Jesus used it on another occasion, He added, "and nothing will be impossible for you" (Matt. 17:20). But Jesus was not speaking here of abstract possibility, but of what was actually going to happen. As Hengstenberg has noted (*Commentary on the Gospel of John*, p. 204), the fig tree that was destroyed by Jesus' word was a symbol of the Jewish people, who faced judgment because of their unbelief (see Luke 13:6-9). In this connection, the mountain also has a symbolic meaning:

So the mountain here is the universal empire that then was, that of Rome. The sea is, according to the common symbolism of Scripture, the sea of nations...out of which the universal empire had arisen mightily in the time of its prosperity, but into which it now sinks back again through the faith of the disciples and the power of Christ. (p. 205)

Thus faith for the casting down of the mountain had its basis in the revelation that promised the triumph of the kingdom of God, as, for instance, Daniel's interpretation of Nebuchadnezzar's vision: "And the stone that struck the image became a great mountain and filled the whole earth" (Dan. 2:35).

Mark 11:24, then, does not contain an unlimited promise that *any* prayer whatsoever will be answered. The promise is qualified by faith, and faith is seen here to rest upon what has been revealed of God's nature and promise. As Lenski says,

Infidelic literalism may challenge a disciple to move a mountain or two and laugh when he is unable to do so; blind fanatics may tempt the Lord to fulfil His word, to do what that word never intended, and may even persuade themselves that their folly has come to pass. But neither of these affects the promise as it stands. God does no silly things, no useless things, none for mere display; yet it is His power that He places behind Jesus' disciples to do the things that He lays upon them as such disciples. (*St. Mark's Gospel*, p. 494)

Faith is not a belief that "anything can happen," but the confidence that what God has promised will happen. In accordance with this, the content of the prayer of faith is determined by what God has promised.

Prayer According to the Will of God

Prayer with submission to God's will, and prayer according to God's will, are not precisely the same thing. In the garden of Gethsemane, Jesus prayed, "Not as I will, but as You will" (Matt. 26:39), yet His petition, "Let this cup pass from Me," was not according to His Father's will. Missing in this prayer of Jesus is the confident assurance that His request would be granted, which He expressed at other times (see John 11:41-42).

In contrast to this is the promise of 1 John 5:14-15:

> Now this is the confidence that we have in Him, that if we ask anything according to His will, He hears us. And if we know that He hears us, whatever we ask, we know that we have the petitions that we have asked of Him.

The most significant part of this statement is not that God hears (hearkens to, grants) prayers that are according to His will, but that a believer may know that his petition is heard, and, therefore, can be confident of the answer even before he actually experiences it. But since God acts in accordance with His own will (Eph. 1:11), such confidence can be present only if it is known that the prayer is according to God's will. The "will" of God referred to here, then, must be the revealed will of God. John's meaning may be paraphrased as follows: "When you pray in accordance with God's revealed will, you can know with certainty that God will hear and answer your prayer."

It is clear that the knowledge of God's will has been given through the teaching of the prophets and apostles. It was the confidence of the Jews that in possessing the Law of Moses they knew the will of God (Rom. 2:17-18). Jesus confirmed this when He compared the Jews to a servant who knew his master's will (Luke 12:47). It was a part of Paul's apostolic commission to know God's will, and be a witness of what he had seen and heard (Acts 22:14-15). Accordingly, those who received His instruction received knowledge of the will of God (1 Thess. 4:1-3).

Not all of God's will has been revealed, but the positive teaching of 1 John 5:14-15 is that the content of the prayer to which an answer can be confidently expected must conform to the revelation that God has given in the Scripture concerning His will.

Prayer in the Name of Christ

It is only necessary here to refer to the previous discussion of the meaning of the name of Christ, in which it was shown that "the name of Christ" refers to the fullness of revelation regarding Him (see Chap. 4). To pray in His name, then, involves not only faith in the revelation by which we know Jesus, but "that the petition abide in the circle of that revelation" (Lenski, *St. John's Gospel*, p. 991). Thus in John 14:13, "whatever you ask" is not unrestricted, but is governed by the phrase "in My Name." The promise of an answer is given only to prayer that is in harmony with the revelation that centers in Christ. Again, the content of prayer is regulated by the Word of God.

The freedom from fixed forms in prayer, then, is not unlimited freedom. Whenever the promise is given that God will hear and answer the prayers of His people, the condition is either implied or explicitly stated, "if they are according to the Word of God." Probably no one has stressed this intimate connection between the Word of God and prayer more than Calvin. He says:

> Again, only out of faith is God pleased to be called upon, and He expressly bids that prayers be conformed to the measure of His Word. Finally, faith grounded upon the Word is the mother of right prayer; hence as soon as it is deflected from the Word, prayer must needs be corrupted. (*Institutes*, III:XX:27)

Calvin regards the Lord's Prayer as the summary of scriptural teaching about what may be asked in prayer. Therefore:

> Those who dare go farther and ask anything from God beyond this: first, wish to add to God's wisdom from their own, which cannot happen without insane blasphemy; secondly, do not confine themselves within God's will but, holding it in contempt, stray away farther in their uncontrolled desire; lastly, they will never obtain anything, since they pray without faith... for here the word of God is absent, upon which faith, if it is to stand at all, must always rely. (III:XX:48)

Every proper prayer, then, must be capable of being related to the petitions of the Lord's Prayer.

Degrees of Conformity to the Word of God in Prayer

Three classes of prayers may be distinguished in relation to the principle that the content of prayer is to be regulated by the Word of God, and corresponding to them, three different kinds of expectancy are possible.

There is, first of all, prayer that rests upon explicit commands and promises of Scripture. When a person prays for the forgiveness of sin, he has the command of Christ to pray like this: "And forgive us our debts" (Matt. 6:12), and the promise of John: "If we confess our sins, He is faithful and just to forgive us our sins and to cleanse us from all unrighteousness" (1 John 1:9). James 1:5 authorizes prayer for wisdom: "If any of you lacks wisdom, let him ask God." In such cases, there can be no question that the request is according to the will of God. Therefore, a confident expectation that an answer will be given is justified, is in fact required. To have any doubt in such prayers is to reject the truth of God's Word. In prayer of this kind, as Calvin says, "If we would pray fruitfully, we ought therefore to grasp with both hands this assurance of obtaining what we ask" (*Institutes*, III:XX:12).

A second kind of prayer is that which is known to be in harmony with the Word of God in its intent, but in which the specific features of the request have no explicit basis in Scripture. These are specific requests that rest upon general promises of Scripture. For example, we are commanded to pray for daily bread (Matt. 6:11), and God promises to supply the necessities of life (Matt. 6:30, 33). Therefore, one can be confident in praying that his needs will be supplied, and yet not be certain that a particular felt need (which may not be really necessary) will be met in answer to prayer. To give another example from Scripture: Paul felt that it would be in harmony with the furthering of the kingdom of God if he were to visit Rome, and so he prayed that he might be able to do so (Rom. 1:9-10). Yet he had no revelation from God that it was actually God's will that he go there at that time. So he indicates some uncertainty in his prayer — "by God's will" in this case means, "if it really is God's will." God's will has been revealed in its essentials, but not in all its details: "It is not for you to know times or seasons" (Acts 1:7). "Therefore," Calvin says, "where no certain promise shows itself, we must ask of God conditionally" (*Institutes*, III:XX:12). Prayers about specific events and times and persons, in the absence of specific promises, must always include the proviso "If the Lord wills" (Jas. 4:15). Confidence in such cases rests in the fact that God will accomplish His purpose in wisdom and love, not that a specific request will be granted. Otherwise, there would be the danger of presuming to control God, to bind Him to man's will. In the Lord's Prayer, according to Calvin:

> We are taught not to make any law for Him, or impose any condition upon Him, but to leave to His decision to do what He is to do, in what way, at what time, and in what place it seems good to Him. (III:XX:50)

A third class of prayer is that which has no basis at all in Scripture. James referred to this kind of prayer when he wrote, "You ask and do not receive, because you ask amiss, that you may spend it on your pleasures" (Jas. 4:3). All of the preceding discussion goes to show that in such prayers there is no justification for expecting an answer. Instead, they provoke God's wrath, as is illustrated by the history of Israel:

> They soon forgot His works;
> They did not wait for His counsel,

> But lusted exceedingly in the wilderness,
> And tested God in the desert.
> And He gave them their request,
> But sent leanness into their soul. (Ps. 106:13-15)

There is a special kind of prayer, which seems to belong to this category of prayer that lacks a foundation in the Word of God: the prayer of doubt and complaint. When Job prays,

> *Does it* seem good to You that You should oppress,
> That You should despise the work of Your hands,
> And smile on the counsel of the wicked? (Job 10:3),

he seems to lack faith in God's justice and benevolence. Of course, not every prayer recorded in Scripture is a model which is to be emulated, but the fact that the Psalms, which believers are authorized to use in worship (Col. 3:16), contain expressions of doubt, indicates that such prayers are not always improper. There are a number of reasons why this is so.

First, when believers actually do experience doubt, when they are puzzled about God's dealing with them, it is better to express their real feelings to God than not to pray at all, or to pretend that they have no such feelings. It is to encourage weak Christians to pray that the assurance is given concerning the sympathy of Christ as our High Priest (Heb. 4:15-16). The prayer of doubt is not necessarily devoid of all faith. It is a recognition that God exists, and that He knows the thoughts of the heart. In his trouble, the believer does not turn away from God, but turns to Him, in the kind of prayer that Kuyper calls the "outpouring of the soul." (*Work of the Holy Spirit*, p. 620)

Secondly, it is not inconsistent with true faith in God's mercy to be conscious of God's displeasure. In His love, God chastens and disciplines His children (Heb. 12:6). Therefore, it may well be that for a time His favor is withheld, and His anger is felt. At such times it is appropriate for the believer to pray,

> There is no soundness in my flesh
> Because of Your anger,

> Nor any health in my bones
> Because of my sin. (Ps. 38:3)

At the same time, there is confidence in God's mercy, and a plea for restoration of His favor: "Make haste to help me, / O Lord, my salvation!" (Ps. 38:22).

Finally, in almost every case, in the Psalms, the expression of doubt represents a preliminary stage in prayer—the statement of need. Eventually, there is not only a plea for help, but praise for the answer that has been given. Psalm 73 is an example of such a progression. The prayer of doubt and complaint has its place, then, in so far as it is an honest expression to God of one's inner state, and represents a way of presenting one's need to God and seeking His help. Even though all the sentiments expressed may not harmonize with what is revealed in Scripture, such prayer has for its basis the scriptural truth that the Lord "shall regard the prayer of the destitute, / And shall not despise their prayer" (Ps. 102:17).

Questions for Discussion and Reflection

❧ What has been your understanding of the saying, "Faith can move mountains"? Has it been changed by reading this chapter?

❧ Some teachers on prayer say that to pray "if it be your will" indicates a lack of faith. How do you respond to this?

❧ What connection is made in this chapter between the will of God and the Word of God?

❧ Have there been experiences in your life when you have expressed doubt or complaint in prayer? How do the Psalms help us in such experiences? Which Psalms?

Chapter Eight

The Defense of Prayer

While seeking to give a positive presentation of Scriptural teaching regarding prayer, a theological discussion of prayer must also deal with the objections that have been raised against it. The objections have been many and varied, but the most important of them call into question either the necessity of prayer, or else its efficacy. Generally speaking, the question about the necessity of prayer arises within the framework of belief in the Scriptures, while denial of the efficacy of prayer is the fruit of unbelief.

The Necessity of Prayer

"Objection" may be too strong a word to describe the kind of questioning that arises in the minds of believers about the necessity of prayer. It is a matter of seeking to reconcile what the Scripture teaches about prayer with its revelation about the nature of God. If God is infinitely wise and benevolent; if it is true that "your Father knows the things you have need of before you ask Him" (Matt. 6:8), if He "is able to do exceedingly abundantly above all that we ask or think" (Eph. 3:20), then what good does it do to pray? Will not God do what is best for us whether we ask Him or not?

There are not many who, on the basis of this question, deliberately adopt the position that prayer is to be abandoned. In so far as their faith in God's wisdom and benevolence is genuine, they are impelled to obey God's command that men are to pray, and so they do. Nevertheless, the intellectual problem remains, and no doubt it often has the effect of making prayer more formal and less urgent than it ought to be.

The Scripture nowhere deals directly with this question; it does not explain why God, who knows what we need and is willing to give it to us, commands us to pray for these needs. The fact remains that He does command us to pray, promises to respond when we pray, and indicates that if we do not pray we will not receive (Jas. 4:2). The command to pray is found side by side with the statement that God already knows our needs, and will supply them (see Matt. 6:8-13, 32-33; 7:7-8).

Still, Christians seek reasons why prayer is necessary. One that is commonly advocated, and that seems to give prayer great urgency, is the view that while God is ready and willing to bless men, He cannot unless by prayer they indicate their willingness for Him to do so. S. D. Gordon, a popular evangelical writer on prayer at the beginning of the 20th Century, gives such an explanation:

> Everything that has ever been prayed for, of course I mean every right thing, God has already purposed to do. But He does nothing without our consent. He has been hindered in His purpose by our lack of willingness. When we learn His purposes and make them our prayers we are giving Him an opportunity to act. (*Quiet Talks on Prayer*, p. 54)

Such an explanation makes prayer necessary in the absolute sense—it is something that God cannot do without. Unless people pray, He is unable to accomplish His benevolent purpose in the world. The progress of God's kingdom in the world, and the eternal destiny of individuals is ultimately dependent upon the human activity of prayer: "There are people…in that lower, lost world…who are there…because someone failed to put his life in touch with God, and pray" (p. 195). While this kind of explanation of the necessity of prayer has a strong psychological and emotional appeal, its implications are devastating. It denies the sovereign control of God over His creation and makes events to rest upon the free will of finite sinful men. If the purpose and activity of God did not control events, then all human activity would be meaningless, including prayer. Since many different persons are involved, all acting as free agents, what was accomplished through the prayer of one could be negated by the failure of many others to pray. It would be just as likely—more so, because our wills are "warped and weakened"— that God's purpose would fail as that it would succeed, and hence all prayer would come to nothing.

The Scriptures present a far different view of the relation between the purpose of God and human will. God

> does according to His will in the army of heaven
> And *among* the inhabitants of the earth.
> No one can restrain His hand
> Or say to Him, "What have You done?" (Dan. 4:35)

"A man's heart plans his way, / but the Lord directs his steps" (Prov. 16:9). "It is God who works in you both to will and to do for His good pleasure" (Phil. 2:13). Such passages indicate that God's purpose is sovereign, and that human will is subject to it. The impulse and ability to pray come from God. Thus prayer cannot be said to be absolutely necessary in the sense that events are ultimately determined by it.

Instead, the necessity of prayer is a relative one; it is necessary because it is one of the means by which God is pleased to accomplish His purpose. And it is not difficult to discern the benefits that accrue to believers by virtue of the fact that God chooses to grant His blessings to them in answer to prayer. Calvin suggests six: (1) quickening of our love for God; (2) purification of our desires; (3) stimulation of gratitude; (4) greater appreciation of the kindness of God; (5) greater delight in the blessings received; and (6) greater confidence in God's promises (*Institutes*, III:XX:3).

Belief in God's sovereignty can itself create problems in understanding the necessity of prayer. If God has unchangeably foreordained whatever happens, then how can prayer have any significance? Since God has declared the end from the beginning, and infallibly accomplishes His purpose (Isa. 46:10), then prayer cannot change His plan. Prayer seems, then, to be superfluous.

This kind of question is only a part of the larger problem of the relation between the sovereignty of God and the significance of all human activity. It is just as easy to conclude from the foreordination of God that believing in Christ, or preaching the gospel, or attempting to safeguard oneself from physical harm, accomplishes nothing, as to say that prayer has no effect.

The solution to the dilemma is not to be found by giving to prayer, or any other human activity, a significance and value that is independent of God's plan and activity. If human decisions are regarded as independent from God, then, as has been said, there could be no assurance that prayer would be answered, since God might be confronted with the impregnable resistance of human will. As John Murray has pointed out, if man were able to command "a realm impervious to God's providence, then there would be a realm which His grace could not invade" (*Calvin on Scripture and Divine Sovereignty*, p. 70).

Human activity appears in Scripture, not as the comple-
ment or antithesis of divine activity, but as the means by which
God's purposes are carried out. In his discussion of providence,
Calvin links praying with man's planning for the future and
taking precautions against accident and disease, which the pro-
fane say are useless since God's plan is already fixed. Calvin
repudiates such a view:

> These fools do not consider what is under their very eyes,
> that the Lord has inspired in men the arts of taking counsel and
> caution, by which to comply with His providence in the preserva-
> tion of life itself. (*Institutes*, III:XX:3-4)

So God moves His people to pray in order that He may respond to their prayers, and thus carry out His will. God ordains means as well as ends, and it is this that gives prayer its
meaning.

Paul finds no contradiction between prayer and God's eternal decree. In his most extended discussion of predestination,
where he shows that the salvation or rejection of Israel rests
upon God's purpose of election, he can say, "Brethren, my heart's
desire and prayer to God for Israel is that they may be saved"
(Rom. 10:1). He is confident that God will complete the work
of salvation that He has begun in the Philippians (Phil. 1:6; see
Rom. 8:29-30); and what he is sure God will do, he prays for
(Phil. 1:9-11).

Without attempting to achieve perfect comprehension of
the relation between God's sovereignty and human activity, the
believer must hold firmly to what is revealed in Scripture, namely
that while God "works all things according to the counsel of
His will" (Eph. 1:11). He also responds to the prayer of His
people who pray in accordance with His will. To conclude from
God's sovereignty that prayer is unnecessary is to reason con-
trary to the clear teaching of the Word of God.

The Efficacy of Prayer

In much of recent theological writing about prayer, there is a strong defensive note. It is as though the question were being asked, "Is it still possible to pray?"—with the implication that recent developments in human knowledge have made the practice of prayer, especially petitionary prayer, very questionable. As Heiler says in his famous work on prayer, "For modern thought, dominated by Copernicus and Kant, prayer is as great a stone of stumbling as it was for the enlightened philosophy of the Greeks" (*Prayer*, p. 362).

In many cases the attempt is made to salvage some meaning for prayer while accepting the non-biblical presuppositions of modern thought. It will be the purpose of this section to discuss two of the forms in which the modern attack on prayer has been made; the way in which these attacks have been answered on the basis of modern thought; and then to evaluate the answers from a biblical perspective.

Objections from the Standpoint of Natural Law

In the 19th and early 20th centuries, many writers on prayer felt it necessary to defend prayer in the face of a prevalent worldview that held that all events were determined by the operation of fixed and unchanging natural laws. Charles Hodge devoted more space to this question than to any other in his treatment of prayer (*Systematic Theology*, III, p. 693ff). George Buttrick wrote his book on prayer "in a silent protest against yielding to an unexamined concept of natural law" (*Prayer*, p. 7).

William Adams Brown, long-time President of Union Theological Seminary in New York, offers a very clear presentation of the difficulty for prayer posed by "natural law," and a way of meeting the difficulty that is characteristic of the older liberalism. Brown states the problem in this way:

There is, first of all, the difficulty which grows out of the new conception of the world which science has given us. What room is there in our world of law, where effect follows cause in inexorable sequence, for the direct initiative of God which the saints take for granted? If there be a God at all, is it not reasonable to suppose that he has expressed himself adequately in the laws he has made? What ground have we, then, for thinking that our prayer can make any difference in his activity? (*The Life of Prayer in a World of Science*, p. 33)

While Brown acknowledges that this view of a closed universe of unalterable law is open to question, he assumes its truth for the purpose of his argument, because many people are convinced that it is true. One possible solution is to suggest that human beings, even though completely determined, nevertheless have the experience of creative freedom. That is, they can to an extent manipulate the laws of nature so as to solve their problems and shape their world. And if human beings can do that, why not God?

World of law though it may be, ours is a world in which new things are constantly coming to pass....In countless ways we fashion the raw materials of our world after patterns which our minds conceive. Why, then, should we conclude that man alone possesses this capacity? Shall the power that produced man be less resourceful than the creature it has produced? (pp. 35ff)

Still, it cannot be confidently asserted that prayers are answered "in the way our fathers believed they were answered"—that is, by God's special intervention in the world (p. 131). The main thrust of Brown's argument lies in another direction. Prayer, for him, is not primarily petition, but is "the practice of the presence of God" (p. 38). Prayer is not intended to have any influence upon God, but gives insight into ultimate values and order. Practicing the presence of God

does not mean that we are to put pressure upon God to come where He is not. It means, rather, that we should concentrate our thought on those aspects of life which assure us that He is here already. (p. 91)

In terms of the psychology on which Brown depends, the elements of human personality tend to be in a state of confusion and conflict. In order to restore health, these conflicting elements must be unified by being attached to a higher principle, something that provides a motive, standard, and goal for human life. God serves as such a principle of integration for the one who prays.

> Prayer brings us into contact with God, and God is the only object in the world big enough and lasting enough and worthy enough to serve as the integrating principle of every human personality. (p. 45)

In prayer, God is experienced as the unifying principle, not only of the individual, but of the universe. In prayer one finds freedom from doubt and fear, because he sees a fundamental order and beauty and goodness in the universe that would otherwise be a threat to him (pp. 133ff). Since in prayer a person finds harmony with himself and the world, he is changed, and this change has repercussions in the lives of others. It is thus that one may account for the value of intercessory prayer.

> We lose the true significance of intercessory prayer if we think of it as the means by which we bring to God those for whom we should pray. Rather, it is God's means of revealing to us what He desires for others, so that we can pray for them aright. (p. 144)

In prayer for others, we gain insight into their real needs, and our attitude toward them is changed, so that we go out to serve them. The wider results of prayer are traceable to the enlightenment that comes to the one who prays.

Does such an account of prayer describe anything more than a process of auto-suggestion? Brown answers that it is indeed auto-suggestion, but that while the unbelieving psychologist concludes that prayer is a delusion, the believer sees in the process of auto-suggestion the working of God.

> In prayer we experience genuine creation: new values arise and new appreciations of old values. Granted that we ourselves are the creators of these values and of these appreciations, who is it that made us what we are?...In prayer we become aware of God at work. (p. 144)

To summarize, Brown sees God as related to the world in terms of purposeful activity. There is order and progress in God's working, so that the world moves in the direction of unity in which presently conflicting elements will be brought into harmony. In prayer, people gain insight into the unity that lies beyond the present disorder, and so achieve integration of their own personalities and a harmonious relation to the world. This enables them to see others in a new light, and to act for their welfare. Prayer thus has a social as well as an individual effect. Whether prayer has any objective result beyond this remains doubtful.

Brown's attempt to give a defense for prayer while accepting the view that events in the world are determined by "natural" causes that are not subject to change by God must be judged a failure. From Brown's own standpoint, if the effect of prayer in the world is due to auto-suggestion, then there is no reason why, for example, the voicing of one's hopes and aspirations should not serve just as well as speech that takes the form of prayer. Prayer might still "work" for the unenlightened, but Brown is writing for those who are seeking an intellectual basis for the practice of prayer. Surely if they understand Brown's reasoning, they will conclude that prayer, in its petitionary form, does not work. Rather, prayer is reduced to "the practice of the presence of God," that is, contemplation or meditation. And petition is unnecessary, and really inappropriate, in meditation.

But, more seriously, Brown's explanation of prayer ignores, or contradicts, the biblical view of prayer. It cannot account for Scriptural assertions that prayer can produce effects in the forces of nature, as in the case of Elijah's prayer for rain (Jas. 5:18). Nor can it explain how, for example, Paul could anticipate that through the prayers of people in Philippi he would be freed from prison in distant Rome (Phil. 1:19). The biblical claim that prayer can have results in the physical world, and in the lives of people at a distance, rests upon the reality of the response and activity of the God who is the creator and governor of all causes and effects.

Against the attacks of a "scientific" world view which sees "an uninterrupted natural interdependence between all things and the absolute dominion of the law of cause and effect" (p. 125), the defense of prayer requires the maintenance of a biblical doctrine of providence. Such a doctrine does not regard anything in the world as independent of God. Abraham Kuyper rejected a dichotomy between "natural" and "supernatural," "as though nature is a power that stands over against God with its own forces and laws" (G. C. Berkouwer, *The Providence of God*, p. 208). There is no question of whether God can affect the forces of nature, for those forces are the work of God. Because there is order and regularity in God's working, it is possible to speak of "natural laws." But they are laws of God's appointment, which offer no resistance when He works in new and unusual ways.

When this biblical teaching regarding God's providential activity is accepted, then the attack upon prayer from the standpoint of a "scientific world view" is successfully refuted.

Objection Based upon the Denial that God is Personal

P. R. Baelz has noted in his book on prayer that the disagreement that exists in contemporary Christendom over the appropriateness of personal terminology in speaking of God:

> Christian tradition makes liberal use of the personal language of divine activity and purpose. Reflection on the mysterious being of God compels us to ask whether such language is to be taken seriously or whether it expresses a lingering but persistent anthropomorphism which needs to be radically discounted. (*Prayer and Providence*, p. 7)

For a large part of modern theology, the latter alternative has been chosen. Yet, inasmuch as there is still a desire to live and think within the framework of the Christian church, and since prayer has always been a central part of Christian worship, an attempt is made to give a meaningful account of how prayer "works."

One such attempt is found in the systematic theology of John Macquarrie, a professor, like Brown, at Union Theological Seminary in New York. Macquarrie takes the thought of Martin Heidegger as the philosophical framework of his theology, and thus attempts to interpret God as "Being." God is not a being among others, nor is He (it?) a cause or some kind of basic "stuff" that underlies the world; rather, God is "the condition that there may be any beings or properties of beings" (*Principles of Christian Theology,* p. 103). "Being" is that which "lets be." Hence the person of faith is one who takes "an existential attitude of acceptance and commitment" toward the "letting-be" of "Being" (p. 94).

Within such a framework, prayer cannot be the address of a human person to a divine Person; "Being" is not conscious, and is not capable of acts of will. "We cannot suppose that prayer is a kind of conversation between man and God or that the usual conditions for communication can obtain in this case." Hence prayer becomes "the way by which we can give shape to our deepest desires, aspirations, and concerns, and, as it were, hold them up in the presence of holy Being." This exposure of inward desires has a purifying effect, as some of those desires are seen to be unworthy. But prayer works positively as well as negatively. "Petitionary prayer makes sense if we are committing ourselves to what we are praying for." The effect of prayer is not only psychological:

> It seems to me that without falling into any magical or fanciful notions on the subject, one may readily admit that prayer has repercussions beyond the life of the person or persons who actually

offer the prayer. Let us think for a moment of the prayer for the coming of the kingdom. While on the one hand this prayer may be a strengthening of one's own commitment to Christ's kingdom, may we not also believe that the sincere prayer of faith is a strengthening of the movement of Being itself in its threefold action of creation-reconciliation-consummation? For this, as we have seen, is not something that proceeds just automatically, but something that needs man's free response and cooperation. (pp. 437-440)

Those who pray actually share in the "letting-be" of Being, and thus changes are produced in the world. Petitionary prayer, by this account, becomes primarily an act of commitment by which one participates in the process of the ever greater realization of existence.

A similar view is advocated by Robert Simpson, who has investigated the writings of five of the Fathers on the Lord's Prayer, with the purpose of obtaining guidelines for a restatement of the doctrine of prayer. Drawing upon "process theology," Simpson regards the concept of God as a symbol for "creative activity," which is "that process by which more complex forms of related-being are produced. That is, creative activity is the increasing integration of divergent elements" (*The Interpretation of Prayer in the Early Church*, p. 161). It involves both biological evolution and the development of interpersonal relations. Faith is essentially, "the acknowledgement of the significance of this process as the ultimate value in human life and the consequent commitment to it" (p. 162). The process of increasing integration is enhanced and forwarded by the free participation in it on the part of human beings. Within such a framework, Simpson defines prayer as "that expression of religion which involves a conscious orientation toward creative activity at the human level by which participation in that activity is facilitated" (p. 157).

The key word in this definition is "orientation." As orientation, prayer involves a struggle of wills in which the will of the individual is conformed to the integrative process. Since the orientation is to "creative activity at the human level," it is "orientation to the community." It is not conformity to a transcendent will of God, but to the life of the community of which one is a part, in so far as that life moves toward more complete integration. Prayer is an orientation of *will*, and as such involves commitment. It is not mere "willingness," but a decision to participate. Therefore, prayer "gives that which it seeks...The ideal of Christian prayer involves ultimate commitment and conscious orientation to creative activity through which ultimate human values are realized" (p. 162).

Like Brown, Simpson does not shrink before the charge that prayer is auto-suggestion:

> "Auto-suggestion" may be said to describe one means by which creative activity occurs, as the means by which the ultimate Source of truth, beauty, and value operates at the human level, only if the term is redefined to mean a fresh integration of values and meanings (and power) that are previously present but inadequately related. (p. 171)

Such a view of prayer does not regard God as personal in the sense that He would respond to prayer in an objective way apart from the change of orientation in the one who prays:

> Christian prayer aims not at the conformity of certain powers to human purposes but at the conformity of man to the demands or conditions by which higher degrees of related being may be achieved.

God is the "transcendent Referrent" of prayer in the sense that creative activity is both the object of ultimate commitment and also the ground or source of prayer. Prayer arises from creative activity and is commitment to creative activity (pp. 172; 164ff).

Both Macquarrie and Simpson attempt to reinterpret Christian prayer in terms of modern worldviews that do not claim to have their basis in the revelation of God in Scripture. Prayer is understood by both to be basically an act of commitment to the movement of being, a movement that is either in the direction of more complete existence (Macquarrie), or of a higher degree of integration (Simpson).

It is certainly true that prayer can express commitment. Jesus' words from the cross, "Father, into Your hands I commit my spirit!" (Luke 23:46) was such a prayer. But to make commitment the essence of prayer is to nullify the biblical teaching about prayer, and makes meaningless much of the language of prayer as it has been practiced by the Christian Church through the centuries. If "God" is not a word that refers to "a being," then it is absurd to use terms of personal address in prayer. If there is no Person to respond to prayer, then it is senseless to voice petitions such as those that make up the Lord's Prayer. If prayer is essentially an act of commitment, then the language of most Christian prayer is at best a clumsy circumlocution. If men like Macquarrie and Simpson are right, then the prayers of the Psalter and even the Lord's Prayer ought to disappear from the Church's worship, to be replaced by something that is a mere shadow of prayer.

The teaching about prayer in the Bible cannot be separated from the biblical view of God and the world that is its foundation and context. The defense of Christian prayer cannot be successfully undertaken apart from an acceptance of the biblical revelation as a whole. But when by faith we apprehend God as personal, conscious, active, powerful, and benevolent; when we see the world as created by God, and under God's sovereign control; when we embrace the commands and promises of God concerning prayer as set forth in the Scriptures; then prayer in all its aspects, not excluding petition, becomes a reasonable and meaningful practice.

Questions for Discussion and Reflection

⟡ Why are believers tempted to doubt the necessity of prayer? Have you personally had this problem?

🗡 Why is the answer given by S. D. Gordon to this problem not satisfactory?

🗡 Does the assertion of the chapter that "God ordains means as well as ends" help you to understand the necessity of prayer?

🗡 How does Paul's experience in the storm and shipwreck (Acts 27:21-25; 30-32) help in understanding the relationship between God's sovereign plan and human activity?

🗡 Why is petitionary prayer such a problem for those who do not accept the Bible's worldview?

Chapter Nine

The Summary of the Doctrine of Prayer

On the basis of the preceding study of the teaching of the Scriptures regarding prayer, the following conclusions are set forth as the substance of the Christian doctrine of prayer:

Prayer is human speech addressed to God. It springs from our consciousness of our relationship to God, and is the means by which we express the affections, needs, and desires that arise from that relationship. As such, it includes adoration and thanksgiving, confession of sin, submission, commitment, and petition.

God is not addressed as though He were a man, nor should man be addressed as though he were God. Prayer is, therefore, to be made to God alone. Because God exists in three Persons, prayer may be addressed to the Triune God, without further specification, or to each of the Persons. The Father, however, has a distinctive role as the Hearer of prayer, and prayer is ordinarily to be addressed to Him.

❧ By our sin, we are estranged from God, and unable on our own to come to Him in prayer. By His obedience and death on the cross, Jesus Christ has made atonement for the sins of His people, and thereby has given them access to the presence of God in prayer. He continues to act as our High Priest in making intercession for the saints, pleading before the throne of God for their full salvation, and powerfully helping them in all their needs. Although believers before His coming into the world did not enjoy as clear a knowledge of His mediatorial work, nor as full an experience of the working of the Holy Spirit as we now have, access to God in all ages has been possible by virtue of His once offering Himself as a sacrifice for sins.

❧ Prayer is impossible for the unredeemed sinner, not only because he is barred from God's presence, but because he lacks the motivation and knowledge necessary to pray aright. The Holy Spirit works in the lives of the redeemed to destroy the power of sin, and to enable them to pray, by giving them spiritual understanding, faith, and love for God and men. Because this work of renewal is not yet complete, the Spirit also assists believers in their weakness by making intercession within them according to the will of God.

❧ As a recipient of the grace of God, the Christian exhibits in praying the qualities of reverence toward the majestic and holy God, sincerity and earnestness, submission to the will of God, faith in what God has revealed concerning Himself and His activity in the world, and obedience to God's commands. These qualities do not merit God's response to prayer, but are evidence that the one possessing them is a child of God, to whom He has given the promise of answered prayer.

❧ God's sovereign will is not subject to control or change by man, and, therefore, God's promise to answer prayer is qualified by the revelation that He has given of His will in Scripture. To pray effectively, one must pray according to what God has promised and commanded in Scripture. Confidence that an answer will be given to prayer is dependent upon the assurance that what is asked has been promised in the Word of God.

❧ The efficacy of prayer does not rest in itself, as though it had some magical power, nor in its subjective effect upon the one who prays. The effects of right prayer are produced by the response of God, who controls all events in the world, who can do all things, who acts in accordance with the counsel of His will, and who hears and answers the prayers of His people.

These conclusions present no finding that can be called new. This is not to say that the practice and teaching of prayer within the Church of the present day conforms to these truths. In particular, the close connection between the content of prayer and the revelation given in the Scriptures is often ignored even within evangelical Christianity. Calvin's strong emphasis upon the fact that prayer must be within the limits of the Word of God, and that the faith that expects an answer to prayer must have its basis in the revelation that God has given of His will, needs to be given new prominence at the present time. In accordance with this, the Church needs to recapture its historical emphasis upon the Lord's Prayer as the paradigm for all prayer. Not only should teaching about prayer be based upon it, but great benefits could be derived from making the Lord's Prayer the structural basis for both private and public prayer. That is to say, in addition to using the Lord's Prayer as an actual form of prayer, its phrases may be used as centers around which the expressions and petitions of free prayer are gathered.

Without claiming to have penetrated fully into the way that the prayers of finite men influence the course of events that is absolutely controlled by the sovereign God, this study has shown that prayer has a place of primary importance in individual piety, and in the accomplishment of God's purpose in the world. It is not that God cannot work unless we pray, but because He has commanded us to pray, and promises to answer the prayer of faith, those whose lives are governed by God's Word and Spirit will be men and women who pray.

Works Cited

Baelz, P. R. *Prayer and Providence.* London: S. C. M. Press, 1968.

Berkouwer, G. C. *The Providence of God.* Trans. Lewis Smedes. Grand Rapids, MI: Wm. B. Eerdmans Pub. Co., 1952.

Bishop, Selma L. *Isaac Watts: Hymns and Spiritual Songs 1707-1748.* London: The Faith Press, 1962.

Brown, William Adams. *The Life of Prayer in a World of Science.* New York: Association Press, 1927.

Brownson, Robert. *Courage to Pray.* Grand Rapids, MI: Baker Book House, 1989.

Buttrick, George Arthur. *Prayer.* New York: Abingdon-Cokesbury Press, [1942].

Calvin, John. *Commentaries on the Epistle of Paul the Apostle to the Hebrews.* Trans. John Owen. Grand Rapids, MI: Wm. B. Eerdmans Pub. Co., 1948.

Calvin, John. *Commentary on the Gospel According to John,* II. Trans. William Pringle. Grand Rapids, MI: Wm. B. Eerdmans Pub. Co., 1949.

Calvin, John. *Commentaries on the Epistle of Paul the Apostle to the Romans.* Trans. and ed. John Owen. Grand Rapids, MI: Wm. B. Eerdmans Pub. Co., 1947.

Calvin, John. *Institutes of the Christian Religion,* 2 vols. (vols. XX and XXI of the *Library of Christian Classics*). Ed. John T. McNeill, trans. Ford Lewis Battles. Philadelphia: The Westminster Press, [1960].

Cochran, Arthur C., ed. *Reformed Confessions of the 16th Century.* Philadelphia: The Westminster Press, 1966.

Delitzsch, Franz. *Commentary on the Epistle to the Hebrews,* 2 vols. Trans. Thomas L. Kingsbury. Grand Rapids, MI: Wm. B. Eerdmans, Pub. Co., 1952.

Godet, F. *Commentary on the Gospel of John,* 3rd. ed., II. Trans. Timothy Dwight. New York: Funk & Wagnalls, 1886.

Gordon, S. D. *Quiet Talks on Prayer.* New York: Fleming H. Revell Company, 1904.

Heiler, Friedrich. *Prayer.* Trans. Samuel McComb. London: Oxford University Press, [1932].

Hengstenberg, E. W. *Commentary on the Gospel of John*, II. Edinburgh: T. and T. Clark, 1865.

Hodge, Charles. *Systematic Theology*, III. Grand Rapids, MI: Wm. B. Eerdmans Pub. Co., 1952.

Jeremias, Joachim. *The Prayers of Jesus.* Naperville, IL: Alec R. Allenson, 1967.

Kittel, Gerhard, ed., *The Theological Dictionary of the New Testament*, II, III, V. Trans. and ed. G. W. Bromiley. Grand Rapids, MI: Wm. B. Eerdmans Pub. Co., [1964, 1965, 1967].

Kuyper, Abraham. *The Work of the Holy Spirit.* Trans. Henry de Vries, New York: Funk & Wagnalls, [1900].

Lenski, R. C. H. *The Interpretation of St. Mark's Gospel.* Columbus, OH: The Wartburg Press, [1946].

Lenski, R. C. H. *The Interpretation of St. John's Gospel.* Columbus, OH: Lutheran Book Concern, [1942].

Lewis, C. S. *Mere Christianity.* London: G. Bles [1952].

Macquarrie, John. *Principles of Christian Theology.* New York: Charles Scribner's Sons, [1966].

Murray, John. *Calvin on Scripture and Divine Sovereignty.* Grand Rapids, MI: Baker Book House, 1960.

Murray, John. *The Epistle to the Romans*, I. Grand Rapids: Wm. B. Eerdmans Pub. Co., [1959].

Murray, John. *The Heavenly, Priestly Activity of Christ.* London: Westminster Chapel, 1958.

Schroeder, H. J. *Canons and Decrees of the Council of Trent.* St. Louis, MO: B. Herder Book Company, 1941.

Simpson, Robert. *The Interpretation of Prayer in the Early Church.* Philadelphia: The Westminster Press, [1965].

Tillich, Paul. *Systematic Theology*, III. Chicago: University of Chicago Press, [1967].

Warfield, B. B. *Biblical and Theological Studies.* Ed. Samuel G. Craig. Philadelphia: Presbyterian and Reformed Pub. Co., 1952.

For Further Reading

Carson, D. A., ed. *Teach Us to Pray: Prayer in the Bible and in the World.* London: Paternoster Press and Baker Book House, [1990].

Goodwin, Thomas and Palmer, Benjamin. *What Happens When I Pray? and Profiting from Prayer.* London: Grace Publications Trust, [1997].

Guest, John. *Finding Deeper Intimacy With God: Only a Prayer Away.* Grand Rapids, MI: Baker Book House, [1992].

Henry, Matthew. *Method of Prayer, with Scripture Expressions; Directions for Daily Communion with God.* Greensville, SC: Attic Press, [1988].

Kistler, Don, ed. *The Puritans on Prayer* (John Preston, *The Saint's Daily Exercise*; Nathaniel Vincent, *The Spirit of Prayer*; Samuel Lee, *Secret Prayer*). Morgan, PA: Soli Deo Gloria Publications, [1995].

Schaeffer, Edith. *The Life of Prayer.* Wheaton, IL: Crossway Books [1992].